"Keith Missel's Bible teaching and pastoral wisdom were instrumental in my personal growth as a Christian. *Living Clay* brings together over a decade of his personal journey of discovery and transformation through engaging with the biblical metaphor of God as the Master Potter. In this eight-week study, you also have the opportunity to learn from Missel's journey and benefit from his sharp pastoral and theological insights as you engage with God's Word. May God, the Master Potter, use it to shape you into the image of His Son."

—Keith Williams, senior editor for Bibles and Bible Reference,
Tyndale House Publishers

"Slow down! Look around! See what God is doing in and through your life. This eight-week devotional study centers on how our God works on us as a potter shapes the clay. The reflections for each day will encourage you. At times you will weep in joy and hope and later find yourself prompted to repent and bow in humility. Keith writes with the Bible and his heart wide open. Join him!"

—Dr. Roy King, professor of ministry leadership,
Columbia International University

"Keith Missel does an excellent job of unpacking the biblical image of Potter and clay and applying it to the Christian's daily walk. His devotionals have a great balance of Scripture and stories, text, and take-aways. The themes presented—from understanding our created uniqueness to recognizing God's sovereignty—are essential for honoring God and living life to the full."

—Dr. John Cionca, executive director of Ministry Transitions Inc., professor emeritus of ministry leadership at Bethel Theological Seminary

"Reading through *Living Clay*, I sense the heart of a pastor who desires to see his people being conformed to the likeness of Jesus Christ. Although replete with strong biblical teaching and a plethora of illustrations and quotations, the book is not 'preachy.' It is written in a warm, nurturing style that invites readers to seek after God and in so doing, allow Him to touch every aspect of their being and change it for His glory and their good. It is a joy to see a former student pressing on to assist people in allowing the Potter to shape their lives."

—Donald L. Hamilton, professor of preaching, emeritus,
Columbia International University

"I am reminded that the Lord pours out His spirit on us. It is such a joy to see the way He molds and makes us into His image. He has poured His love and spirit in this 'earthen clay vessel.' I trust God will use this study and time of reflection to demonstrate how you, too, are being made into *Living Clay*."

—Diane Brown, potter

"It doesn't take long as a follower of Christ to realize that the Father's ways are different from ours. It takes faith, however, to accept that they are higher (Isaiah 55:9). In *Living Clay*, Keith reassures us that we are in good hands. Those hands are relentlessly committed to molding us into the shape of His Son, and that process can be quite rugged in our lives, but Keith reminds us they are wise, firm, and tender hands. Listen to what the Potter has to say to you through this book. I heartily recommend it!"

—Rich Miller, president of Freedom in Christ Ministries, USA

"Dr. Keith Missel has clarified the majestic process of life and ministry from the Potter's perspective. Born out of Keith's personal experience, *Living Clay* is a masterpiece of discipleship that is deeply biblical and very experiential. If you are longing to become the one-of-a-kind work of art the Potter intends, I highly recommend reading *Living Clay*. Purpose to place yourself on the Potter's wheel, like Keith has, and experience the spiritual transformation of life in the Master's hands."

—Don Matthews, certified church health consultant,
The Legacy Consulting Group

"This is a book you cannot afford to miss. Like Jeremiah so long ago, we are invited by God to go down to the Potter's house. Journey there with Keith Missel and the insights will be astounding. You will find answers to the deepest issues of life and you will learn what it means to live in the hands of the Master."

—Larry Magnuson, president of SonScape Retreats

Living Clay

Experiencing a Beautiful Life in the
MASTER'S HANDS

Keith Missel

NEW HOPE®
PUBLISHERS
Gospel-Centered. Missions-Driven.

Birmingham, Alabama

New Hope® Publishers
PO Box 12065
Birmingham, AL 35202-2065
NewHopePublishers.com
New Hope Publishers is a division of WMU®.

Library of Congress Cataloging-in-Publication Data

Names: Missel, Keith, 1959- author.
Title: Living clay : experiencing a beautiful life in the master's hands /
 Keith Missel.
Description: Birmingham, AL : New Hope Publishers, 2016.
Identifiers: LCCN 2016020056 | ISBN 9781625915054 (sc)
Subjects: LCSH: Christian life. | Clay—Miscellanea.
Classification: LCC BV4501.3 .M576 2016 | DDC 248.4—dc23 LC record available at
https://lccn.loc.gov/2016020056

ISBN-13: 978-1-62591-505-4
N174104 • 0916 • 2.5M1

Dedication

To Ellen, my wife and best friend. Thank you for
honoring the dream of writing Living Clay. Over the past three
decades, the Master Potter has used you in so many ways to
shape me into the image of His Son Jesus Christ.
For that gift, I am deeply grateful.

CONTENTS

Acknowledgments

Every book is a team effort and *Living Clay* is no exception. I wish to thank the following for their contributions to my inspiration and knowledge in creating this book:

To the five potters: Diane Brown, Ohio; Robert Alewine, Tennessee; Barb Dreyer, Minnesota; Kristy Downing, Minnesota; and Lucas Magnuson, Colorado; who welcomed me into their studios and tutored me in the art of shaping clay. Your friendship, support, and tutelage greatly impacted my understanding of the Master Potter and how He so wonderfully relates to and works with the clay.

To the family of God at Friendship Church in Minnesota. Your ongoing encouragement provided the necessary wind to keep *Living Clay* sailing through to completion. It is a privilege to serve as your lead pastor.

To Mom, for always cheerleading and believing God's best for your son. Like Christ, your love and support has been unconditional.

To Mark, Sarah, and the team at New Hope Publishers. My experience with New Hope has been exceptional. I feel extremely indebted to you all.

To the Master Potter—thank You, Father, for Your relentless effort to shape the clay of my life for Your glory and my good through Your Son, Jesus Christ.

Introduction

TRANSFORMED
How God Shapes Us for His Glory and Our Good

While I was on a missions trip to Romania, God birthed a passion in me to explore and understand more fully one of the most familiar metaphors in Scripture: the potter and the clay. On this particular adventure, our missions team spent two weeks sharing Christ with students and adults throughout the community of Balș, Romania, with the goal of planting churches in the region of Oltania. One of the cultural highlights took place when our team visited a master potter, Gregorio, in a village called Oboga. As we approached the potter's home, we noticed potsherds and pottery scattered everywhere. The courtyard had large and small vases, uniquely shaped goblets, bowls, cups, and saucers, some ready to sell, others needing to be recycled.

Gregorio looked unimpressive. However, his mature and stately persona gave our team the impression we were going to experience an artistic and cultural treat. Known throughout Romania as a premier craftsman, Gregorio's practice of molding and shaping pottery had endured beyond 60 years. Gregorio sat comfortably at a rugged, old bench fitted just for him. His leather apron kept his trousers and sweater clean. He rolled up his sleeves and prepared to shape the clay. As he engaged the mechanical foot wheel underneath his bench, which slowly turned the wheel on the table, the artist within became visible. Gregorio took a rough lump of clay and placed it on the small, worn wheel. After wetting both hands, he started working the clay with grace and mastery. Within minutes a vase began to appear. As our team gazed on with undivided attention, Gregorio stopped the wheel. With great precision he began removing hardened particles of grit from the clay vessel. He did this numerous times in order to purify the content of the clay. This reminded me of many similar situations in my own life. My dentist, when cleaning my teeth every six months, says, "Tartar hides and must be cleaned out to prevent cavities."

Likewise, my neighbor, a fanatic gardener, will say, "All of these weeds have to be pulled from the flowerbed or else their roots will eventually kill the good plants." Obviously, life's impurities need to be extricated, no matter what the circumstances.

What took place next with Gregorio, however, affected me dramatically. After spending much time shaping and molding a beautiful vase, he stopped the wheel again. He locked both his hands and placed them together on top of the vase. Then, with great accuracy and force, Gregorio crushed the clay vessel back to the wheel. *What just happened? I wondered in shock. The piece being shaped looked really nice. Why are you starting over? Seems like a waste of time and energy!*

Then God's Spirit brought clarity as I sensed Him saying, "Keith, this is a picture of what I, the Master Potter, have been doing with you during the past 20 years: shaping you into the image of My Son." What stuck with me was less the crushing of the pot and more the potter's process—in the hard and the good of life, when things were gloriously flourishing or in times of pain and confusion, God was molding me to be a vessel of use for His purposes. Tears began to flow, and time seemed to stand still. No one on our team knew how precisely, yet tenderly, God was speaking to me in the moment. It was a divine encounter. The impression the Potter made that night has lasted more than a decade. It launched a quest in my soul to grasp more fully the majestic ways of the Potter, which has culminated in the writing of this book.

Desiring to portray a potter's work accurately, I spent more than a year getting to know numerous artists in the states of Minnesota, Ohio, Tennessee, and Colorado. Some of these were divine appointments. On a trip to the North Shore in Minnesota, my wife and I stopped at a coffee shop in the small town of Grasston, just north of the Twin Cities. We noticed beautiful pottery crafted by a lady named Barb Dreyer. Her business card read, "His creation, my inspiration." I felt compelled to call Barb. Since then, Barb has tutored me in the art of hand building, the art of making pottery without a wheel. She has invited me into her studio to experience her work firsthand.

We all know the delight of being taken into care by a mentor. Some of us can remember a shop teacher from high school who helped us build our first birdhouse or bookcase, which led to a lifetime of enjoying woodworking. Some of us had grandmothers who instilled a love for cooking and baking by letting us help make the Thanksgiving turkey or the Christmas pie. No matter what our age may be, we value the time others invest in us, and Barb certainly has been an influential mentor to me. Through Barb and others, I have discovered that the community of potters is gracious and very willing to open their lives and share knowledge. These potters have become friends and have taught me more than I could ever reciprocate. In addition, I have done my best to handle correctly the metaphor of Potter and clay by anchoring it in theological truths that flow directly from the context of Scripture. This book is more than devotional reflections; it is a robust examination of this important figure of speech scattered throughout the Old and New Testaments. Nearly 2,700 years ago God told Jeremiah, "Go down to the potter's house, and there I will give you my message" (Jeremiah 18:2). I'd like to invite you, as God did Jeremiah, to join me at the potter's house, so we can hear from Him regarding these timeless truths.

WEEK 1

HIS HANDS: *Living the Unique You*

On the whole, God's love for us is a much safer subject
to think about than our love for Him.
—C. S. Lewis

Day 1
The Master's Hands

My first real experience with clay took place in the fall of 2012 at Diane Brown's studio in Morrow, Ohio. I remember how excited I was to sit under her tutelage and get my hands into the clay. I was as thrilled as a child learning to ride a bike. Diane's workshop, which her husband, Mike, had set up on the main floor of their beautiful country home, was quaint yet functional and accessible. Diane strategically positioned her wheel in the corner of her studio where two windows provided natural light. After she oriented me to the dynamics of throwing clay, she inquired, "Are you ready to create?"

Because I had little understanding of throwing clay, I initially felt apprehensive. I strapped on a cloth apron and sat awkwardly, huddled around the wheel. After wedging the mud (throwing the clay down in such a way as to remove air bubbles and prepare it), I followed Diane's instructions and slammed the clay on the middle of the wheel. The first and most important step of centering the clay perfectly on the wheel is much harder than it looks. Like people, every lump of clay has a unique personality. My first lump of clay earned the name of "obstinate." Feelings of frustration came over me as it resisted my efforts at centering. With Diane monitoring my progress, I finally centered the clay. While in the process of shaping a simple bowl, I can still hear her loving reminder: "Keith, keep your hands on the clay." Because of fatigue, I abandoned the lump of mud on the wheel. Diane told stories of how centrifugal force can cause neglected clay to lose center, become distorted, and even fly off the wheel. For the remainder of that day, I became very conscious of keeping at least one hand firmly on the clay.

The ultimate lesson I learned that day is that the potter's chief tools are his hands. The prophet Isaiah wrote, "Yet you, LORD, are our Father. We are the clay, you are the potter; we are all the work of your hand" (Isaiah 64:8). How encouraging for the clay to know that the Potter's hands are always on us and actively working.

Read the following passages. How do they demonstrate that God's hands are always on us, actively shaping the clay of our lives?

Psalm 121:1–4

Philippians 1:6

Romans 8:28–29

As a Christian for more than three decades, I can attest to this reality. The Potter's hands have never abandoned me but have continued to form, shape, and mold me into the unique and useful vessel He desires. At times, we may doubt His ongoing work. We may not feel or sense His gentle and purposeful touch. However, we must remember the promises of God to stand firm. David shared this sentiment when he wrote, "The LORD will vindicate me; your love, LORD, endures forever—do not abandon the works of your hands" (Psalm 138:8).

Consider the story of Joseph. As a young man of 17 years of age, his brothers hated him and sold him as a slave.

Read Genesis 39. In verses 1–5 and 21–23 what phrase is repeated in the life of Joseph?

For over a decade, Joseph experienced some incredible trials as a slave and then as a prisoner in Egypt. However, God turned Joseph's circumstances around, and in Genesis 41 we read that Joseph was promoted to a position of authority over all of Egypt.

Read Genesis 41. In what ways do you see the hands of God shaping Joseph during his years as a slave and a prisoner to prepare him for leadership?

Our lives, then, are not subject to some invisible force or blind fate; our lives are in the hands of a Person—the Almighty Potter. God is not just our Creator, He is our Father, and He has a personal concern for our lives, just as a potter has a vested interest in the clay. Therefore, God is ever at work, designing and forming, shaping and molding, glazing and painting, ultimately to fire vessels of honor fit for His use.

Scripture relentlessly reveals the divine activity of the Potter's hands on the clay. Clearly, God wants us to understand the workings of His durable but gentle hands. One thing is for sure: when you examine the potter's hands, you will see the residue of clay. Mud literally fills every gap under the fingernails and clay powder occupies every pore of each hand. Other tools are important, including the potter's wheel and table, as well as the shaping, rolling, cutting, and finishing devices, but make no mistake about it—the hands of the potter are his primary instruments.

Write out a prayer of appreciation to the Potter for how His loving hands are molding and shaping you.

_____

_____

_____

_____

_____

_____

_____

_____

_____

_____

_____

_____

Day 2
Hands of an Artist

O ur Heavenly Potter is, first and foremost, an artist. The first few chapters of Genesis vividly describe the artistry of God by recounting the creation of Adam.

••

Read Genesis 2:7. What words identify God as an artist?

••

The Hebrew word for "formed" is *yatsar*, which describes "one who constructs clay, earthen objects and containers." In the ancient world, *yatsar* also described skilled craftsmen, known as artisans, who worked primarily with their hands. In some cases throughout Scripture, for instance in Isaiah 29:16 and Jeremiah 18:4 and 18:6, potter and creator are used interchangeably to describe God's ingenious handiwork. However, the Potter's ingenuity did not end with the creation of Adam.

••

Look up the following Scriptures where the same Hebrew word *yatsar* (translated *create*, *formed*, *made*, *Creator*, etc., depending on the version) is used and describe in detail the specific handiwork of God.

Genesis 2:19

Psalm 104:25–26

Isaiah 45:7

Isaiah 45:11–12

Jeremiah 1:5

••

Many passages throughout Scripture remind us that the Lord's artistic relationship to His creation and chosen ones is analogous to the relationship of the potter to the clay (Isaiah 64:8). Because God is an expert artisan, any lump of clay can become a treasured creation. In its natural state, clay has no obvious value, use, or worth. However, in His artistic hands it can become an object of incredible significance. No other book in Scripture more graphically depicts the artistic activity of God than the memoirs of Jeremiah. In its opening chapter, the Potter reveals to the prophet the sovereign purpose for which Jeremiah was created. In chapter 18, the Artisan's house becomes the venue from which the prophet hears God's message. In chapter 19, the Potter explicitly communicates His intentions toward the nation of Israel by demolishing a clay pot and drawing spiritual parallels for Jeremiah to declare to his kinsmen. Jeremiah's life provides a visual aid for how the artistic hands of *yatsar* will shape and mold an individual for kingdom assignments.

From Jeremiah 1:4–5, identify four terms God uses to show His involvement in Jeremiah's birth and life.

God_____ Jeremiah.

God_____ Jeremiah.

God _____Jeremiah apart.

God_____ Jeremiah as a prophet.

What can we learn from this passage about God as Potter and Creator?

I have a friend that attended a ministry school in Minnesota who felt pressured to respond to an imposed missionary "calling" by the institution. The school seemed to promote that God's will and spirituality was tied to going overseas. Anything less would be a failure. However, he heard a liberating message emphasizing that God's calling is unique for each one of us and no one calling is more important than another. It took some time for him to get over the guilt of not fulfilling his "missionary" mandate. However, today he is a husband, father, elder in a local church, and works as a self-employed contractor to the glory of God.

In this passage *Yahweh* communes with the one He intends to commission (Jeremiah 1:4, 11, 13). The Potter's revelation to Jeremiah includes the striking and attention-getting repetitive word *before*. God wants Jeremiah to recognize that *before* he was formed, the Potter already knew him, and *before* his mother gave birth, the Craftsman already set him apart. In Jeremiah's case, his birth and his vocation were conjoined because his call was, as Jack R. Lundbom states, "ordained from eternity."

•••

Is Jeremiah's "before" calling unique to Jeremiah alone, or is his life an example of a beautiful pattern established throughout Scripture?

Describe the particular calling of the Lord on the following individuals:

Abraham (Genesis 12:1–4)

David (Psalm 78:70–72)

Esther (Esther 4:13–14)

Mary the mother of Jesus (Luke 1:26–35)

Paul (Galatians 1:15)

Have you discovered God's unique calling on your life?

•••

Day 3
Artistic Hands Shape Relationally

......

Read Jeremiah 1:5a. What does it mean that God knew Jeremiah before He formed him?

......

The Potter used three verbs in Jeremiah 1:4–5 to describe his imaginative efforts in Jeremiah's life, and they set the stage for understanding the Potter's handiwork with the clay. The first verb depicting the Potter's creativity is the Hebrew word *yada*, which is translated "know." According to Thompson in *The Book of Jeremiah*, *yada*, however, "reached beyond mere intellectual knowledge to personal commitment." For Jeremiah, *yada* involved God initiating a personal and intimate relationship with him that would sustain the prophet through many difficult and painful experiences and allow him to fulfill his God-given calling. The prophet Amos used *yada* to reflect on Yahweh's relational commitment to Israel. The New Living Translation expresses God's passion for His people, saying, "From among all the families on the earth, I have been intimate [*yada*] with you alone" (Amos 3:2).

......

Read 1 Chronicles 28:4–7. In verse 6, what endearing term does David use to describe the relationship between his son Solomon and the Lord?

Read Ephesians 1:4–5 and **Romans 8:15–16.** How does recognizing God as your Father influence your relationship with Him today?

......

The Eternal Potter is closely connected and personally committed to the clay. He understands the nature of the clay, which insures the shapeless lump of mud will become a vessel for worthwhile use. Because of this intimate knowledge, a potter gives special attention to the specific properties of the earth, including the clay's porosity (the existence of minuscule openings or spaces within the clay), shrinkage (when the amount of clay decreases in size due to drying and firing), plasticity (a quality that allows clay to be shaped and molded without cracking), and firing temperature (the hardening and strengthening of ceramic materials through heat). These qualities, called the clay body, are inherent to the composition of the clay's nature and are known to the potter.

Our Master Potter knows us intimately before the clay of our lives ever gets placed on the wheel. He understands the unique and special attributes of each type of clay. He discerns how much pressure the clay can handle and how hot to heat the kiln for firing. Because the temperament varies from clay to clay, the Potter will tailor-make each vessel accordingly.

Like godly parents who long to train up their children according to their leaning or bent, God personally and intimately fashions us according to the unique disposition of our clay.

A friend of mine recently visited Europe with his wife. While walking through a museum, their tour guide related this story: Michelangelo was once asked how he was able to create such amazing sculptures. He replied that when he looked at a block of granite, he saw an angel trying to get out. So, he merely chipped away all of the rock that prevented the angel from being exposed and released. To us, the granite block would be ugly and useless, but to a master craftsman such as Michelangelo it was a potential element of beauty. So, too, are we in the eyes of God.

Knowing about the mud's composition nevertheless still involves a personal and relational affection between the potter and the clay. The book of beginnings uses *yada* to describe sexual intimacy between Adam and Eve (Genesis 4:1). Both testaments depict the marital union as the most explicit symbol for God's bond with His people (Hosea 3:1; Ephesians 5:21–33).

••

Write out the following verses:
Isaiah 54:5
Isaiah 62:5
Jeremiah 2:1–2

What is the common theme among these passages?

••

Both Isaiah and Jeremiah evoke the emotional response of joy and elation that a man experiences on his wedding day and throughout the early years of marriage. The first time the marriage metaphor between God and His people is fully explored is when the Lord asked the prophet Hosea to marry a prostitute. Yes, as crazy as it sounds, God used a relationship between a godly servant and an ancient call girl to depict His marvelous and relentless love toward us. Jud Wilhite comments in his book, *Pursued: God's Divine Obsession with You*, on this strange but powerful command to Hosea:

> When God wanted to illustrate the passion, love, and relationship He desires to have with us, He didn't showcase a lawyer with a bureaucratic list of "do's and don'ts." He didn't platform a politician who would introduce strategies to change the world. He didn't choose a sword-wielding warrior, a power-hungry monarch, or an invincible superhero. He didn't even choose a saint or a priest. He chose a prostitute.

Read Hosea 3:1. What is God's motivation for commanding Hosea to take such drastic measures?

The pain of having an unfaithful partner is surely one of the most agonizing of all human experiences. It is the ultimate betrayal. Yet, this is how God describes His relationship to Israel. If you ever question the veracity of God's commitment to a covenant love relationship with His people, examine the Book of Hosea and you will discover His heart beating for you "with an everlasting love" (Jeremiah 31:3). Potter Douglas Marks mirrors the same repose in his artistry, saying that the clay is everything to the potter, and from the moment the two touch, there's a lasting connection.

I can only imagine that it shatters God's heart when people miss this essential aspect of the relationship between Potter and clay. For many years, that was my story. I grew up conscious of God but not knowing Him personally. I had religion without relationship. Although I was reared in the church, I never understood that God created me for fellowship and enjoyment. My distorted paradigm relegated God to a cosmic cop who ruled life from heaven with a ten-foot billy club. Step out of line and *whack!* But God's love broke through because He knew me before He formed me and pursued me with a relentless love. I came to experience a true love relationship as a result of coming to know God intimately and personally through Jesus Christ, His Son. The Bible depicts this relationship as a bride and bridegroom that is never ending, for He is always faithful (John 3:29; 2 Timothy 2:13). He longs for a first-love relationship with His people (Revelation 2:4) as the bride prepares herself for the ultimate of wedding celebrations (Revelation 19:7–8). May I encourage you from the outset that the loving relationship between Potter and clay is paramount in understanding this marital metaphor in Scripture?

••••••••••••••••••••••••••••••••••••

Read Jeremiah 9:23–24. According to our Heavenly Potter, what is the greatest prize in life?

Do you know the Lord personally?

Have you relinquished yourself to the hands of a loving Potter, who artistically shapes you according to your bent?

••••••••••••••••••••••••••••••••••••

Day 4
Artistic Hands Shape Uniquely

Write out Jeremiah 1:5.

Read Leviticus 20:22–26. Describe from this passage what it means to be set apart for the Lord.

Read Ephesians 1:1–2. Notice that Paul called the believers at Ephesus saints. Is there a relationship between being set apart and being a saint in Christ?

The second verb in Jeremiah 1:4–5 illustrating the Potter's ingenuity is the Hebrew word *qādaš*, translated as "set apart." The basic meaning of *qādaš* is "to be holy or consecrated," but *qādaš* also emphasizes commitment and expresses concern of setting something apart for limited and specialized use. So, God's choice of Jeremiah to function as a prophet to the nations was the reason he was set apart. His calling had nothing to do with his moral achievements or spiritual attributes.

The fact that the Potter consecrates our lives beforehand is a dimension of our relationship with God that is often neglected or simply forgotten in our more therapeutic and pragmatic twenty-first-century Christianity. Today, we give much attention to family of origin or the antecedents of chaos or stability that bear us along in this life. Although these dynamics are influential and should not be discounted, the Master Potter reminds the clay that our true selves are much more divinely given to us than they are naturally formed by us or our surroundings. Jeremiah's uniqueness was not set in motion by his parents, the social stratum he came from, the band of brothers he grew up with, or the Ivy League school he attended. No, the Bible does not say much about these supposed formative venues; however, it does say much about the Artist—what the Maker was doing and how He consecrated the clay before it was actually placed on the wheel.

Like Jeremiah, our uniqueness begins with God. If we take God out of the equation, then Kerry Livgren of the band Kansas was right: all we are is "Dust in the Wind." In 1977, this classic hit became the band's highest-charting single ever, reaching #6 on the *Billboard* Hot 100 chart. This incredibly popular folk song struck a chord about our longing for answers to life's ultimate questions. Jeremiah's Creator wanted him to know that before he took his first breath, God was the answer to life's most perplexing questions. Because Jeremiah is consecrated by God, he is unique and exclusively positioned to fulfill God's specific plan.

Kristi K. Downing told a story about a gentleman who requested that she make identical pieces of pottery for him and his twin brother. Kristi did everything in her power to replicate the process from one creation to the other. Although, in some regards, the pieces came out similar, they also came out unique. Just as in the world of pottery, no two people are alike because God handcrafts each one exceptionally for His glory.

Recently, I asked friends on social media to share their favorite Psalms and express why it brought inspiration and support to their lives. I was delighted to discover that Psalm 139 got high ratings. One individual referenced Psalm 139:7–17 and stated that this passage helped her heal from her childhood. Another friend wrote that Psalm 139 became the inspiration for a book he is currently writing. My daughter shared with me that Psalm 139 has always been her favorite, especially verses 13–14, which state, "For you created my inmost being; you knit me together in my mother's womb. I praise you because I am fearfully and wonderfully made; your works are wonderful, I know that full well."

••

What picturesque words did David use in Psalm 139:13–14 to describe God's unique creation?

God _____ David together in his mother's womb.

David was _____ and _____ made by God.

God's works are _____ .

••

According to author Roger Ellsworth in his book *Opening Up Psalms*, by using the term *knit*, David "pictures himself as a fine piece of art and God as a skilled craftsman." The Potter's goal is to create a spectacular work from each lump of clay.

••

Read Ephesians 2:10. How does the Apostle Paul describe us humans to the believers at Ephesus?

••

The Greek term for workmanship is *poiēma*, which literally means "something that is made," a work of divine creation. The New Living Translation calls this divine formation God's "masterpiece."

A spectacular example of a potter creating a one-of-a-kind piece came to light recently in London, England. While cleaning out their parents' home, a brother and sister discovered an eighteenth-century Chinese porcelain vase. At auction, the vase ended up selling for a world-record-breaking $69.3 million (£43 million). Both the auctioneers and the siblings were stunned when the 16-inch porcelain vase that was imperially commissioned from the Qing dynasty went for what is believed to be the highest price of any Chinese artwork sold at auction. Helen Porter of the auction house described the vase as "a piece of exquisite beauty and a supreme example of the skill of the ceramicist and decorator." The auctioneer's website said the piece "would have resided, no doubt, in the Chinese royal palace and was most certainly fired in the imperial kilns. It is a masterpiece."

God, the Artist, formed Jeremiah to live as His extraordinary and matchless work of art. What was true of Jeremiah is true for all who are shaped by God through Jesus Christ. How disturbing to think that many people today feel much like the American novelist Ernest Hemingway, who said:

> **Life is a dirty trick, a short journey from nothingness to nothingness. There is no remedy for anything in life. Man's destiny in the universe is like a colony of ants on a burning log.**

Hemingway's inability to understand God's unique design for his life led to suicide at age 62. Sadly, many today follow in Hemingway's footsteps. According to the American Foundation for Suicide Prevention, suicide is the tenth leading cause of death in North America, with more than 40,000 individuals taking their lives each year and an average of 12.93 suicides per 100,000 individuals. This unfortunate reality reminds us how vital it is to gain God's perspective on our existence. Every life must be treasured as unique and priceless.

Never forget that every book has a creative author, and every work of art reflects an artist. Before God formed Jeremiah, He set him apart for unique and noble purposes. Human beings are included in a grander scheme because we are part of the purposeful achievements of God.

The inspirational life of Sue Thomas wonderfully illustrates how the Potter shapes the clay uniquely. At 18 months old, Sue became deaf. However, this lifelong disability prompted a career as a Federal Bureau of Investigation agent, where reading lips helped crack crimes and bag the bad guys in places listening devices could not penetrate. She believes that her deafness gave her a platform to share her faith and opened the door to many unique opportunities for ministry. In 1990, she published her autobiography, *Silent Night*. The acclaimed book became the basis for the TV series *Sue Thomas: F. B. Eye*. In 2002, the first episode appeared on PAX Television and became one of the two highest-rated shows on the network. The viewership grew to 2 million people in the United States, and the show has aired in 54 countries around the world.

This remarkable, edge-of-your-seat drama is a tribute to the Potter's masterful work with His clay and should inspire us to realize that we are the work of His hands. What if every individual engaged life as Sue Thomas did and embraced his or her uniqueness for the glory of God?

According to a world population website, as of April 2, 2016, there were 7,412,779,574 people living on planet Earth, which included more than 289,000 babies born that day. However, each individual was and is exceptional because the Creator hand builds everyone and puts His image and likeness on every person (Genesis 1:26–27).

I have identical twin boys. Even though, at times, friends and family mistake their identity because of their outward appearance, it is very clear to my wife and me that our two sons are radically unique. Their individuality began in the mind of the Potter because He already knew them before He formed them (Jeremiah 1:4–5). At conception, the DNA composition of their clay was providentially fixed, resulting in two very special, one-of-a-kind works of art. That is why King David sang, "I praise you because I am fearfully and wonderfully made; your works are wonderful, I know that full well" (Psalm 139:14). Max Lucado reflects this sentiment when he writes:

Da Vinci painted one *Mona Lisa,* Beethoven created one Fifth Symphony, and God made one version of you. You're it! You're the only you there is. . . . Can you be anything you want to be? I don't think so. But can you be everything God wants you to be? I do think so. And you do become that by discovering your uniqueness.

If you ever doubt your worth or value in this life, may I encourage you to come back to the Potter's words to Jeremiah, remembering that before you were born God set you apart as a one-of-a-kind work of art? Grow to discover His unique fingerprint on your life. Embrace His "before" work the way the prophet Jeremiah and Sue Thomas did. He made you you-nique and longs for you to reflect His glorious creation to others (Ephesians 2:10).

Write a prayer of thanksgiving for your unique qualities and the ways God uses His shaping for kingdom causes.

_____

_____

_____

_____

_____

_____

_____

_____

_____

_____

_____

_____

Day 5
Artistic Hands Shape Purposely

....

Write out Jeremiah 1:5.

....

The third verb in Jeremiah 1:4–5 describing the Potter's originality is the Hebrew word *nâthan*. This refers to the "specific assignment" the Potter had prepared for His clay. Numerous passages in Scripture use *nâthan* to describe God's distinctive assignments for His people.

....

Read Genesis 17:1–8. Describe in your own words God's ministry assignment for Abraham. From what you know about Abraham's life, did he fulfill this assignment?

Read Exodus 7:1–2. How does God describe His ministry assignment to Moses?

From what you know about Moses, how well did he fulfill God's call?

....

Every potter will tell you clay is always shaped according to the artist's will, and each vessel has an exclusive purpose. Diane Brown told me that her stimulus for creating pottery comes in real time. In the morning she may envision the creation of a planter or candy dish. However, in the afternoon, inspiration prompts her to craft a mixing bowl or a teapot. This innovative process of designing is the potter's privilege. Jeremiah's appointment to serve as prophet came without any dialogue or consultation. Even before the Potter began wedging the raw material of the clay, He already had in mind what the clay of Jeremiah's life would look like and become. God expressed to Jeremiah that His divine intention for the prophet reached back before his birth. The Potter wanted the prophet to know that his kingdom assignment was preplanned. Jeremiah's exclusive task involved serving as a prophet to the nations, beginning with his own people in Judah. His comprehensive charge spanned four decades of ministry, and his work involved a dedication to going wherever and to whomever God called.

The Bible is replete with examples of God shaping His people for ministry "before" other elements weighed into the equation. The Lord chose Abram out of the clay pit of pagan Mesopotamia and shaped him to bless all the nations of the earth (Genesis 12:1–3). God took the marred clay of a murderer and fugitive named Moses and then molded him into a redemptive leader (Exodus 3–4). The Potter selected Samuel from his mother's womb to guide Israel in the ways of the Lord (1 Samuel 3:1–21). In a vision where he experienced the glory and call of God in an unprecedented way (Isaiah 6:1–13), Isaiah reflected on his divine invitation, saying "Before I was born the LORD called me; from my mother's womb he has spoken my name" (Isaiah 49:1). God's handiwork evidenced itself in the resolute life of Esther, who served as queen and ultimately saved the nation of Israel from genocide (Esther 8:1–17). The Potter launched the ministry of John the Baptist by filling him with the Holy Spirit "even before he [was] born" (Luke 1:15). Paul told the Galatian church that God "set [him] apart from [his] mother's womb" so that he "might preach him among the Gentiles" (Galatians 1:15–16). From his comprehensive review of Scripture in the book *Jeremiah and Lamentations*, author R. K. Harrison concluded that:

> **There is nothing haphazard about the choice of Jeremiah as a divine messenger to Israel. Indeed, God had formulated each step of the process Himself from conception to consecration, with an intimate awareness both of the need and the one who should meet it.**

Write out John 15:16.

Why did Jesus say He chose His disciples?

Read the following passages about the Apostle Peter. How does Peter's life demonstrate a fruitful and God-honoring lifestyle?

John 21:15–19

Acts 2:14–41

Acts 12:1–19

1 Peter 5:1–4

Living Life on Purpose

By 2009, *The Purpose Driven Life* had sold more than 52 million copies and has been translated into more than 50 languages since its release in 2002. It was described as the bestselling nonfiction hardback book in history. In a Barna survey of American pastors and ministers, *The Purpose Driven Life* was identified most often for having the greatest influence on their lives and ministries. Amazing! We can only conclude that the popularity of this monumental work demonstrates how deeply people long to know God's plan for their lives. It is a fact, Craig Groeschel submits in his book, *Chazown*, that, "Everyone ends up somewhere but few people end up somewhere on purpose." How tragic, because God intends all of us to live full and meaningful lives like Jeremiah did. Our resolute existence originates with God, who declares, "I make known the end from the beginning, from ancient times, what is still to come. I say, 'My purpose will stand, and I will do all that I please'" (Isaiah 46:10).

Saul of Tarsus came to understand the divine aims of God. Although he studied under Jerusalem's finest scholars, zeal trumped knowledge and prompted his persecution of Christ's church (Philippians 3:6; Acts 8:1). But God's grand ambitions prevailed when Saul had a personal encounter with the risen Savior. His vision of Christ on the road to Damascus dramatically recalibrated his spiritual GPS. While sharing his testimony with King Agrippa, the transformed apostle declared that he was "not disobedient to the vision from heaven" (Acts 26:19). Paul ended up "somewhere on purpose" because he aligned himself with God's "before" plan for his life.

For many years I've been privileged to help Christians discover their particular calling by offering unique classes such as Body Life or Discovering Your SHAPE for life and ministry. At times, we find the idea of discerning God's "calling" for our lives a bit daunting. In one setting I remember a lady saying, "I don't believe I have anything special to offer the Lord and His church." As my wife and I continued to probe and help her work through the Body Life material, the lightbulb came on and this lady said, "Do you think God could use my cleaning business?" After some creative conversation she committed her cleaning company to periodically detailing our church. What a beautiful discovery and what a wonderful gift to local ministry purposing to reflect God's kingdom. For this woman, considering the ways that she could use her gifts, passions, abilities, and experiences to serve the local church was just the first step in the larger journey of discovering what unique kingdom purposes He created her to do.

A few years ago, the leadership team of our church engaged our congregation in discovering its unique calling and God-given purpose. Our leadership read *Kingdom Assignment* by Denny and Leesa Bellesi. Through this inspirational work, God reminded us that He calls us to live as contributors, not consumers. During a worship service, our teaching pastors challenged the congregation to trust God to lead them to a tailor-made mission. At the close of the morning message, the pastors offered individuals $50 of seed resources and asked them to discern prayerfully how God would have them invest and multiply these resources. During the next several months, one God story after another surfaced as the Lord led His people to specific kingdom assignments. Each task derived from the individual's passion and God-given abilities.

Some of these kingdom assignments became long-term ministries. For instance, a few families in our church are now partnering with a ministry, known as Breaking Free, in St. Paul, Minnesota. Breaking Free rescues women from the tragic lifestyle of sex trafficking, which the United Nations estimates is a $32 billion industry and the Federal Bureau of Investigation says is the fastest-growing business of organized crime on the planet. In the fall of 2013, the leadership of Breaking Free served as the keynote speaker for our missions conference. Discovering our kingdom assignment produces much fruit for the glory of God.

Day 6
The Work of His Hands—Nick Vujicic

Are you inspired or skeptical about being clay in the Potter's hand? Do you wonder if you can find your relational rhythm with the Creator of the universe? Still questioning if your life can have purpose or if you are truly uniquely and wonderfully made? If so, consider the extraordinary life of Nick Vujicic (pronounced VOO-ye-cheech). Try imagining what it must have been like to be created without arms or legs. God designed Nick uniquely in that way. In 1982, he was born in Melbourne, Australia, to Pastor Boris and Dushka Vujicic. Shocked, his parents had no forewarning that their son was limbless in his mother's womb. Nick's birth would test the genuineness of their faith. Their trial included seasons of denial, hurt, and disillusionment. Nick's parents often wondered how their son could live a normal life, given his massive debility. However, over time they came to love, accept, and appreciate their precious child for how God had shaped him.

At an early age, Nick developed proficiencies in computer games, swimming, and skateboarding, and he never let his disabilities limit his growth. Through a combination of technology and sheer willpower, Nick faced his physical challenges head-on. However, Nick's struggles went far beyond his physical limitations. He remembers the teasing and feelings of inadequacy on his first day of kindergarten. He cried throughout the day, not wanting to attend school. He dealt not only with bullying and self-esteem issues but also with depression and loneliness. He constantly questioned why he was different from all the other kids surrounding him; why was he the one born without arms and legs? He wondered what the purpose behind his life was or if he even had a purpose.

As Nick grew up, people would ask him, "What happened," but he had no answers, and according to the doctors there was no medical explanation. His parents reminded Nick that only God ultimately knew why. With time, Nick began to embrace his unique and extraordinary situation. However, his real turning point took place at age 15 when he put his faith in Christ as his Savior and Lord. Nick testifies how God's

Word broke through and brought hope in the midst of confusion. While reading the Gospel of John, Nick learned about a man who had been born blind. As people inquired about the "why" of this tragedy, Jesus responded that his disability came about "so that the works of God might be displayed in him" (John 9:3). That truth dramatically influenced Nick's worldview. All his life he just wanted someone to comprehend what he was going through, and now he realized Jesus truly understood. The personal application of that story changed Nick's life forever. He came to believe that Jesus had formed him in his mother's womb for a reason and that he was fearfully and wonderfully made (Psalm 139:14).

When asked how he perseveres through difficult days, Nick encourages people to take "one day at a time with Jesus." By embracing the grace and gospel of God, Nick has become a testimony to what the Potter can do with surrendered clay. On his website, lifewithoutlimbs .org, Nick says, "If God can use a man without arms and legs to be His hands and feet, then He will certainly use any willing heart!"

Nick reminds us that the plans of God stand firm. At the age of 19, Nick began sharing the good news of Jesus Christ through motivational speaking and his testimony, and by 21 he was sharing with people all around the world. In 2007, he relocated from Brisbane, Australia, to California, United States. Today he serves as the president and CEO of a nonprofit organization, Life Without Limbs. Ultimately, because the Potter's hands were always on Nick, this courageous clay vessel now says he "found the purpose of [his] existence, and also the purpose of [his] circumstance."

It is absolutely true that the Potter's most important tools are His hands. His hands shape us for a relationship that is unique and purposeful. His hands never leave us or forsake us. Are you experiencing that intimate, matchless, and resolute relationship with the Master Potter? Can you embrace the words of Isaiah and declare, "Yet you, Lord, are our Father. We are the clay, you are the potter; we are all the work of your hand" (Isaiah 64:8).

Father,
Thank You for Your loving and creative handiwork
in my life. Help me to comprehend how I can have
a relationship with You and experience Your gracious and
ongoing touch. May I never settle for religious experiences
when I can enjoy the intimacy of Your love through Jesus Christ.
Show me how to respond to Your love with all my heart, mind,
soul, and strength. Help me, Lord, to discover and fulfill
Your unique plan for my life. In Jesus' name, I pray.
Amen.

WEEK 2

....

SURRENDER: *The Serenity of Surrender*

JEREMIAH 1:4–19

If my life is surrendered to God, all is well.
Let me not grab it back, as though it were in peril in
His hand but would be safer in mine!
—Elisabeth Elliot

Day 1
Tough Callings

Robert Alewine, who has thrown clay for more than 40 years, describes terra-cotta as defiant. Because the potter puts the clay through conditions it does not want to experience, the clay naturally resists the potter's efforts. Therefore, bringing the clay to complete surrender is the ongoing work of the potter and the necessary response of the clay.

In his book *Bruchko*, Bruce E. Olson tells his remarkable story and demonstrates how valuable pliable and surrendered clay is in the Potter's hand. At age 19, Bruce completely relinquished his life to the Potter as he left his family and friends in Minnesota to serve in Colombia, South America. Olson humbly submitted to God's call, even after being rejected by missions agencies who viewed him as an outsider because he was too young and inexperienced.

As he yielded his life to the will of God, the Lord provided the courage he needed to enter the northeastern jungles of Colombia known as Motilandia in 1961. No white man had survived contact with the isolated and hostile Motilone people in 400 years of recorded history. His initial efforts to share the love of Christ led to his capture, disease, terror, torture, loneliness, and almost his very life. However, after years of building bridges and learning their language, Bruce experienced the joy of seeing the Motilones embrace the gospel of Jesus Christ.

God called the prophet Jeremiah to a life of surrender, much as he did Bruce Olson. He summoned Jeremiah to serve among his countrymen, who were hostile and, for the most part, opposed his efforts.

....

Read Jeremiah 1:11–19. Describe, in your own words, God's tough calling on Jeremiah's life.

....

Try putting yourself in Jeremiah's sandals. You grew up among an idolatrous people who turned their backs on God. God commissions you, saying, "Go, tell the people of Judah that I am going to punish them and their land, unless they repent. You will plead with them to change, but they will not." And, by the way, Jeremiah, "they will mock and persecute you. Many years of preaching will have little spiritual impact." (See Jeremiah 7:26–27.)

........··..............................··.........

What emotions might you feel toward this tough calling? Check every one that applies.

☐ Fear ☐ Encouragement ☐ Blessing

☐ Excitement ☐ Indifference ☐ Zeal

☐ Anger ☐ Frustration ☐ Apprehension

☐ Joy ☐ Special ☐ Privilege

☐ Discouragement ☐ Panic

Why might you struggle with surrendering to this call?

........··...............................··.......

Scripture makes it clear that there exists a dynamic relationship between the Potter and clay. Therefore, the clay's response to the Potter really matters. Clay can fight and become hardened or yield and become pliable. That is why Scripture declares, "Today, if you hear his voice, do not harden your hearts" (Hebrews 3:7–11). In this passage, today is a rhetorical device emphasizing how urgent it is for the clay to surrender. The Potter wants us to know that hardened clay is worthless. And He wants to show us the purposes for which He made us. And make us into the vessels that He intended.

In 627 BC, the people of Judah were resistant to the will of God. They desperately needed a prophetic word to soften the clay of their hearts. The Master Potter graciously began shaping his young servant to deliver that message. During approximately 40 years on the Potter's wheel, Jeremiah, the prophet known for his constant weeping, learned how to yield his life and ministry to the Lord. In this graphic and honest memoir, we will discover how the prophet learned to surrender all and become useful clay in the Potter's hand.

....

Read Jeremiah 1:4–8. What fears did Jeremiah encounter as he processed God's call on his life?

We all have tough callings in our lives that may prompt fear or apprehension in doing His will. These tough callings could include raising a special needs child, dealing with health issues, loving an unbelieving spouse or a wayward child, a challenging work environment, a ministry that is struggling to survive, or a financial calamity. Take a moment to describe your current challenge and identify any fears that hinder you from embracing these tough callings.

Take time to pray, sharing with God your specific struggles and fears. Ask Him to help you embrace your tough calling and move forward for His glory.

....

Day 2
Surrender Your Fear

Right from the start, the Lord acknowledged Jeremiah's trepidations head-on by telling him not to dread his divine calling. Jeremiah's fears were real and needed examination. Jeremiah was not alone in his fears. He reflects the continual cry of inadequacy among God's servants as he expressed apprehensions regarding God's call on his life.

Scripture is replete with examples of God's people struggling to embrace the call on their lives. Consider the response of the prophet Moses as God directed him to confront Pharaoh and deliver Israel from Egypt.

Read Exodus 4:10–12. How did Moses initially respond to this unique calling?

What particular fear did Moses experience?

Have you ever encountered a time where fear hindered the will of God in your life?

In *Courageous Leadership*, veteran pastor Bill Hybels addresses how fear immobilizes those in leadership:

> Sometimes I ask pastors who are grieved because their churches are dying, "Why haven't you introduced change?" I ask business leaders who are hesitating to launch a new product, "Why haven't you taken the step?" I ask political leaders who are waffling on issues they claim to feel strongly about, "Why haven't you taken a public stand?" Often the response is: "Because I'm afraid."

Being no stranger to fear of failure, I can identify with these leaders. Although more than 25 years have passed, I can vividly remember my first ministry assignment as a youth pastor in Cincinnati, Ohio. After serving for nearly a year, the dread of failure paralyzed me to the point of hospitalization. The severe, ongoing pain in my stomach resulted in medical treatment that included an upper and lower gastrointestinal exam. Thankfully, my problem related only to performance anxiety. I will always remember the doctor's counsel: "Keith, once you start thinking right you will start feeling better." Worry produced a psychosomatic illness that paralyzed me in ministry for a season.

Clearly, God's servants are not alone in their fears. Mark Twain said, "The human race is a race of cowards; and I am not only marching in that procession but carrying a banner." Nobel Prize winner Albert Camus called his era "the century of fear." Through his alter ego, Charlie Brown, Charles M. Schulz addressed his phobias head-on, saying, "I have a new philosophy. I only dread one day at a time."

Fear can, indeed, be crippling. Soldiers in battle sometimes become so overwhelmed by terror, bloodshed, and carnage, they experience a situation called battle blindness. Although there is nothing physically wrong with their eyes, their brains will not process any new images of combat. These warriors go blind and stay that way until they are removed to safe places and allowed months or even years to regain their confidence and again start to see.

In his memoirs, *It Worked for Me: In Life and Leadership*, General Colin Powell entertained a question from an honest 13-year-old girl from Japan. "'Are you ever afraid?' she asked. 'I am afraid every day,' she continued. 'I am afraid to fail.'" The general responded, "I'm afraid of something every day, and I fail at something every day. Fear and failure are always present. Accept them as part of life and learn how to manage these realities."

Jesus recognized the epidemic of fear among humanity and aggressively tackled the topic by urging His disciples to not be afraid (John 14:27; Luke 12:7, 32) and to "take heart" (John 16:33).

Not only did Jesus acknowledge the prevailing disposition of fear and exhort His followers to a better way, but He also demonstrated that overcoming fear is a spiritual battle. In preparation for Calvary, Jesus prayed through the early hours of the morning in Gethsemane. Jesus agonized and sweat drops of blood (Luke 22:44), crying out, "'Abba, Father,' he said, 'everything is possible for you. Take this cup from me'" (Mark 14:36).

••

When Jesus prayed, "take this cup from me," what was He actually asking from His Father?

Does it seem strange that in His humanity, Jesus struggled to embrace the Cross and requested His Father to consider a plan B?

What can we learn from Jesus' prayer in Gethsemane on how to address our fears?

••

Day 3
The Powerful Presence of God

Read Jeremiah 1:4–6. What two concerns did Jeremiah have with embracing God's call in his life?

Interestingly, both of Jeremiah's fears related directly to how people would respond to his leadership and areas that he viewed as personal weaknesses. I'm sure Jeremiah wondered, *How can such a young person perform such a formidable task?* Although no one knows Jeremiah's exact age, scholars suggest his call came during his teenage years or, at the latest, in his early twenties.

Jeremiah's dread demonstrates his vulnerability; surrendering one's life to the Potter is a risky proposition. Think about it: take Jeremiah off the Potter's wheel and remove this tough calling; he now moves forward in life alleviating some of these dangers or hazards, and, therefore, some of his concerns vanish.

On the flip side, when a person is centered in the Potter's hand and yields to God's request, it often includes peril, challenge, and danger that may produce anxiety and restlessness. Our church supports missionaries that serve in "high-risk" ministry environments where bombings, threats, and crisis are ongoing realities that produce added pressure, anxiety, and depression. However, they labor, like Jeremiah, to stay centered on the Potter's wheel and move forward with their tough calling.

Thankfully, the Potter knew the composition of the clay and supported Jeremiah in dealing with his fears. Fear is not wrong or sinful in itself. Fear is simply an emotional response to real or imagined danger. In fact, the Word of God assumes that we will periodically encounter the emotions of fear and anxiety. In Psalm 56:3 David wrote, "*When I am afraid, I will trust in you*" (author's emphasis). However, God's Word never portrays our fear simply as an emotion over which the believer has no control. The biblical imperative not to fear is a command never to panic or become paralyzed by one's fear.

••

In Jeremiah 1:8 God provides the antidote for the prophet's dread stating, "Do not be afraid of them, for I am with you and will rescue you." What reason does God tell Jeremiah not to be afraid?

••

God reminds Jeremiah that fear is not ultimately the issue but rather how fear and trepidation are dealt with. God assured Jeremiah that he could trust in the Potter's presence and power to overcome all fear. Trusting in the Lord is the antidote to all fear.

Both testaments develop the truth that God's powerful presence supports us in living victoriously over our phobias. Take a moment to reflect on the repeated promises that describe how God assured His servants that they could trust Him regardless of the situation.

••

Read the following passages and describe, in your own words, the promises God made to these individuals and how those assurances supported their unique callings.

Genesis 26:3

Joshua 1:9

Judges 6:16

Acts 18:9–10

••

David Livingston, known as the "apostle to Africa," demonstrated how vital God's powerful presence is for ministry. As a young man he surrendered to the Lord's summon and prayed, "Lord, send me anywhere, only go with me." Livingston's prayer became his mantra as he engaged the continent of Africa in the mid-1800s with the gospel of Jesus Christ. God's powerful presence was enough to settle all fear, worry, suffering, and loss. After penetrating the interior of Africa, the Scottish missionary returned to his homeland and was invited to speak at the University of Glasgow. Dr. James Kennedy, in his book *What If the Bible Had Never Been Written?*, recounts the exploits of this great missionary and invites us to take a front row seat and listen in on this lecture given over a century ago:

Livingstone came to the platform with the tread of a man who had already walked 11,000 miles. His left arm hung almost uselessly at his side, his shoulder having been crushed by a huge lion. His body was emaciated, his skin a dark brown from 16 years in the African sun. His face bore innumerable wrinkles from the ravages of the African fevers that had racked his body. He was half deaf from rheumatic fever, and half blind from a branch that had slapped him in the eyes. He described himself as a "ruckle of bones."

The students stared in disbelief . . . They knew that here was a life that was sacrificed for God and fellow man. They listened while Livingstone told them about his incredible adventures; he told them about the extraordinary needs of the natives of Africa.

He said to them, "Shall I tell you what sustained me in the midst of all of these toils and hardships and incredible loneliness? It was a promise, the promise of a Gentleman of the most sacred honor; it was this promise, 'Lo, I am with you always, even unto the end of the world'" (Matthew 28:20). That was the promise, that was his text, that was the secret of Livingstone's commitment. It was the presence of Jesus Christ with him everywhere, all of the time.

That promise grasped the heart and mind of Livingstone and transformed his life.

When we walk in the shadow of the Almighty, no task will seem too great, no dilemma too confounding, and no hardship too burdensome. In order to yield to God's will, we have to surrender our fears by trusting in the Lord with all our heart. J. Hudson Taylor, the founder of China Inland Mission, boldly reminds us, "All God's giants have been weak men who did great things for God because they reckoned on His being with them."

....

Look back to Day One of this week and your checklist response to tough callings. How does God's promise that He will be with you impact your progress in fulfilling His tough calling?

How does His powerful presence help you overcome any spiritual inhibitions that may limit His work in your life?

....

Day 4
Surrendering Your Future

In addition to surrendering his fears, the Master Potter called Jeremiah to relinquish his future. Like any young man, Jeremiah possessed hopes and ambitions. I can imagine Jeremiah envisioning landing that perfect job and enjoying the good life. Dreams of marrying a godly, "Proverbs 31" woman, and being blessed with a quiver full of children undoubtedly filled his heart.

....

Read Jeremiah 16:1–2. What did God command Jeremiah to relinquish?

....

These mandates were countercultural and would have caused any servant of the Lord to second-guess his or her calling. For a Jewish man to have no offspring was unthinkable and culturally disgraceful. The family name lived on through one's progeny, which provided hope in the present and for the future.

....

Does Jeremiah's tough calling sound unfair or maybe even cruel?

What does this tough calling teach us about God and about what ultimately matters in life?

....

Surrendering Your Security

Americans place a premium on living secure lives. After 9/11, our country created a department called Homeland Security. One of the top priorities of the George W. Bush administration was to secure the borders and protect the American people from terrorism. As stated in his book, *Decision Points*, President Bush believes his most meaningful accomplishment as president, after the horror of 9/11, was seven and a half years without a successful terrorist attack on American soil.

Yet, as the Potter shaped the prophet for ministry, He seemed to strip Jeremiah of all his earthly securities in order to create an attitude of complete surrender (Jeremiah 11:18–23; 12:6).

....

Read Jeremiah 11:18–23. How did the residents from his own village of Anathoth treat Jeremiah?

....

Talk about terrorist attacks. God revealed the scheming and diabolical plans of Jeremiah's enemies. The conspiracy against Jeremiah that threatened his security thickened, and God personally warned His prophet, saying, "Even your brothers, members of your own family, have turned against you. They plot and raise complaints against you. Do not trust them, no matter how pleasantly they speak" (Jeremiah 12:6 NLT).

....

Not only was Jeremiah's village and family against him but the spiritual leaders of his day were also against him. According to Jeremiah 26:7–8, how did the prophets and priests respond to Jeremiah's message in the Temple?

....

Can you see the treachery forming against God's servant? His enemies camped all around him, and they included his own blood relatives. Jeremiah had very little support in life and ministry. He faced the potential of feeling lonely and incredibly insecure about his service to the Lord.

For those of you called by God to frontline ministry, take courage from Jeremiah's plight. Ministry is difficult and not for the weak-kneed. Recently, an elder, who planned on attending Bible college and serving as a pastor to his village in Mali told me, "I cannot take the ridicule and scorn from my family and friends. The Christian life is too hard." Although our team addressed persecution head-on when communicating the gospel, the intense derision from his Muslim community pushed him to abort the Christian faith. It broke our team's heart.

Regardless of the specific calling, those who serve the Lord for any length of time will experience a Judas in their life. I will never forget at my ordination service in 1987, my mentor in ministry said, "Keith, beware, because a time will come when some of your closest friends and colleagues will turn on you in ministry." How sobering a statement to a young and zealous pastor fresh out of Bible school.

King David bemoaned the disloyalty of his "companion and close friend" (Psalm 55:12–14). The Apostle Paul understood betrayal. In the final days of his life, he wrote about antagonists and deserters among his own ministry team. Demas, a co-worker in the gospel, deserted him. All in Asia forsook him (2 Timothy 4:9–22). Some of you reading this book have been rejected by family members and friends because of your faith and service to Christ. Take heart, because that is part of taking up the cross and following the Savior.

....

Read Luke 12:51–53. How did Jesus describe the cost of true discipleship and the potential impact on those we love most?

....

On January 11, 2013, I got a small taste of what Jeremiah experienced as he relinquished his security. Less than 18 hours before our team would leave for Mali, West Africa, the news headline shouted, "Malian president declares state of emergency." This cry for help compelled France to deploy 2,500 troops and air strikes. The mission: thwart the efforts of rebels who had ties to al-Qaeda militants. The United States State Department issued travel warnings. A barrage of emails, phone calls, and text messages all suggested our team should abort the mission because of the unrest. As team leader, I immediately called each team member. "It looks like we may cancel our missions trip because of the state of emergency," I told them.

Our group met the following morning at 8:00 a.m. to discern God's will. I intentionally woke at 3:00 a.m., which is 8:00 a.m. Malian time. To prepare for our meeting, I made several calls to in-country leaders, which included a staff sergeant from the Malian army. Our team met to pray, discuss, and most importantly to hear from God. One individual said, "Tell us what you think, pastor. We trust your decision." After I presented the facts as best as I could discern them, we made a conference call to a veteran missionary. Pete had served in Mali for the past 13 years. His insights helped tremendously. We committed to honor one another's decision to stay or to go. We cried, prayed, and shared our hearts. Many months of preparation had gone into the trip. Four villages were anticipating our ministry partnership. One individual shared his devotion that morning from Psalm 121. Through that Psalm, God began to speak with incredible clarity.

> I lift up my eyes to the mountains—where does my help come from? My help comes from the LORD, the Maker of heaven and earth. He will not let your foot slip—he who watches over you will not slumber; indeed, he who watches over Israel will neither slumber nor sleep. The LORD watches over you—the LORD is your shade at your right hand; the sun will not harm you by day, nor the moon by night. The LORD will keep you from all harm—he will watch over your life; the LORD will watch over your coming and going both now and forevermore.

His living and active Word prompted an experience of His manifest presence. More tears were shed as we gave testimonies about how family members were also struggling with our decision. A mother and father agonized about leaving their two children behind. However, as we shared our hearts, all said they had to go to Mali and would trust the Lord for their safety and their future. That morning, God taught us, like He did Jeremiah, about trusting in the Lord with all our heart. We were reminded that our security did not come from the state department, the Malian government, or the French army. During our ministry among the villagers, one Malian leader said to me, "We knew you cared for us. Now we know you love us." God used the safety concerns of Mali to advance His work and gospel in a powerful way. We all learned to trust in the powerful presence of our Lord. Alan Redpath helps us embrace why God, at various times, strips away our security when he writes, "The best place any Christian can ever be in is to be totally destitute and totally dependent upon God, and know it." On that trip to Mali, our team absolutely knew Whom we were trusting in.

Day 5
Surrender Your Reputation

....

Read Jeremiah 18:11–12, 18. How did the people respond to Jeremiah's message, and how did they try to destroy his reputation?

Have you ever had your reputation unjustly tarnished? In that difficult situation, how did you respond?

....

The Potter now calls Jeremiah to surrender his name and status. I can only imagine what it must have been like for this young preacher to hear God say, "They will not listen to you; when you call to them, they will not answer" (Jeremiah 7:27). As a pastor, I have a hard time when a few people doze off any given Sunday morning. Last week, some of you fell asleep during your pastor's message, and he went home a bit discouraged. Not only did the people of Judah refuse to listen to Jeremiah, but they also mocked him as a doomsday prophet (Jeremiah 8:14). In addition, God often put Jeremiah in awkward environments by calling him to utilize a variety of unusual graphics while communicating. For instance, while appearing before King Zedekiah (son of Josiah), he wore an ox's yoke on his shoulders, warning Judah and the surrounding nations of the coming bondage to Babylon (Jeremiah 27:1–22). Though his message was serious, the men around him could only see how ridiculous he appeared. Jeremiah surrendered his reputation and learned to live as a God-pleaser, not a man-pleaser.

....

Read Matthew 5:10–12. How does Jesus encourage those who suffer for righteousness' sake, like Jeremiah did?

Jeremiah reminds us that in every age those individuals who represent God to a depraved world will face hardship.

So, where do you find your security?

Do you put your hope and trust in the support of family, friends, and reputation?

Are you known more as a man-pleaser than a God-pleaser?

···

We need to embrace the perspective of the psalmist when he wrote, "Some trust in chariots, and some in horses: but we will remember the name of the LORD our God" (Psalm 20:7 KJV).

Surrendering Your Results

As difficult as this truth may be to embrace, God called Jeremiah to surrender the fruit or results of his ministry to the Lord. As clay in the Potter's hands, Jeremiah needed to learn that faithfulness, not performance or results, is the final litmus test of ministry. God made it clear to Jeremiah that his preaching would fall on deaf ears: "When you tell them all this, they will not listen to you; when you call to them, they will not answer" (Jeremiah 7:27). How frustrating it would be to know that your labor for God would produce very little fruit, at least not as contemporary ministries measure results.

Further, three times God instructed Jeremiah not to pray for his kinsmen because his prayers would have no impact whatsoever, for God would not listen (Jeremiah 7:16; 11:14; 14:11). Jeremiah's pleading, preaching, and praying would not accomplish spiritual transformation. In fact, God told Jeremiah that Israel's heart would harden, not soften, and things would go from bad to worse. They would pattern themselves after their "stiff-necked" ancestors, who perished before the Lord in times past (Jeremiah 17:23; 19:15).

I have periodically wondered how I might react to that kind of commission. Communicating to deaf ears would frustrate any young, aspiring preacher, and Jeremiah was no exception. Few of us would joyfully accept a calling like Jeremiah did. Some of us would probably wonder if God knew what He was doing. Others would simply refuse to obey. Jeremiah, however, grew to embrace God's call because, as clay in the Potter's hand, he learned to relinquish ministry results to God.

Most of us cannot imagine entering a career doomed for failure. In a society that equates success with achievement and accolades, it takes a mature person to say yes to God's call regardless of the outcome. Yet, Jeremiah learned surrender and yielded to God's plan by agreeing to a life of faithfulness that left the results up to God. Oswald Chambers, a man deeply respected for his commitment to Christ, boldly declared, "Our call is not to successful service but to faithfulness." One day, every follower of Jesus Christ will stand before the Bema Seat, or Judgment Seat of Christ, and be rewarded for their service to our Lord. Do you long to hear Jesus say, "Well done, good and faithful servant! You have been faithful with a few things; I will put you in charge of many things. Come and share your master's happiness!" (Matthew 25:21)?

••

How would you evaluate your current faithfulness to the Lord?

Is your ultimate goal to live faithfully like Jeremiah and leave the results of your ministry with God?

••

Day 6
Surrender Today

L ike most of us, Jeremiah periodically struggled to surrender his life and ministry to the Lord. Clearly, God called him to a rare work that many would find difficult to embrace. Jeremiah depicts one of his frequent wrestling matches to relinquish his life to the Lord:

> You deceived me, LORD, and I was deceived; you overpowered me and prevailed. I am ridiculed all day long; everyone mocks me. Whenever I speak, I cry out proclaiming violence and destruction. So the word of the LORD has brought me insult and reproach all day long. But if I say, "I will not mention his word or speak any more in his name," his word is in my heart like a fire, a fire shut up in my bones. I am weary of holding it in; indeed, I cannot. I hear many whispering, "Terror on every side! Denounce him! Let's denounce him!" All my friends are waiting for me to slip, saying, "Perhaps he will be deceived; then we will prevail over him and take our revenge on him." —Jeremiah 20:7–10

This passage concludes Jeremiah's ongoing complaints to the Lord; it seems very bitter and has been called his Gethsemane. Jeremiah details his impossible dilemma as he goes all in for kingdom work. If he proclaims truth, his audience becomes angry and rebels all the more. If he remains silent, he disobeys God and lacks inner peace. Jeremiah uses harsh language, accusing the Lord of deception and manipulation in His call. Like many of God's servants who struggle to submit their will to the Lord, the prophet reminds us that God can handle our complaints and discouragements.

....

Why do you think Jeremiah accused God of deception?

Was Jeremiah accurate in his complaint? Did God mislead him? (See Jeremiah 1:8, 19; 12:6.)

Have you ever struggled like Jeremiah to understand why a life of obedience would result in such hurt, pain, affliction, and trial?

....

Could it be that one of the greatest hindrances to relinquishing the clay of our lives to the Potter is the suffering that results from being a vessel of honor fit for the Master's use? Years ago, during an evening prayer meeting, an elderly woman passionately prayed, "It really doesn't matter what You do with us, Lord. Just have your way with our lives." That night, Adelaide Pollard, a rather well-known itinerant Bible teacher, attended the prayer meeting very discouraged because she had been unable to raise the necessary funds for missionary work in Africa. Deeply moved by the older woman's prayer, Adelaide went home and reflected on Jeremiah 18:2–4:

> "Go down to the potter's house, and there I will give you my message." So I went down to the potter's house, and I saw him working at the wheel. But the pot he was shaping from the clay was marred in his hands; so the potter formed it into another pot, shaping it as seemed best to him.

Before retiring that evening, Adelaide Pollard completed the writing of all four stanzas of the hymn "Have Thine Own Way, Lord."

> Have Thine own way, Lord! Have Thine own way!
> Thou art the potter, I am the clay.
> Mold me and make me after Thy will,
> While I am waiting, yielded and still.
> Have Thine own way, Lord! Have Thine own way!
> Search me and try me, Master, today!
> Whiter than snow, Lord, wash me just now,
> As in Thy presence humbly I bow.
> Have Thine own way, Lord! Have Thine own way!
> Wounded and weary, help me, I pray!
> Power, all power, surely is Thine!
> Touch me and heal me, Savior divine!
> Have Thine own way, Lord! Have Thine own way!
> Hold o'er my being absolute sway!
> Fill with Thy Spirit till all shall see
> Christ only, always, living in me!

The life of Jeremiah inspires us to let the Lord have His own way. A surrendered life values trust over fear. Relinquishing our future and family means we have confidence in the One who holds our loved ones and our tomorrows in the palm of His hand. When we surrender, our success and security take a backseat to the will of God. It allows us to embrace hurts, ridicule, and disappointments as a means to a God-honoring end. Submission moves us from self-centeredness to God-centeredness as the Potter shapes us into vessels of honor fit for His use. In his book *The Grand Weaver*, Ravi Zacharias reminds us that "at the end of your life [and mine] one of three things will happen to your heart: it will grow hard, it will be broken, or it will be tender." Surrender keeps the clay of our hearts tender, and we must remember that, like every other potter in the world, God only uses soft and pliable clay.

Is there any area of your life that needs surrendering to God?

Is there anything preventing you from moving forward and relinquishing this area of your life to the Lord?

How about closing this chapter and writing a personalized prayer to the Potter expressing your desire to surrender all to Him?

_____

_____

_____

_____

_____

_____

_____

_____

_____

_____

_____

_____

_____

_____

WEEK 3

CENTERED: *Are You Too Restless to Rest?*

EXODUS 20:8–11

*God, you have made us for yourself, and our hearts
are restless till they find their rest in you.*
—Augustine

Day 1
Leading On Empty

....

Read Exodus 20:8-11. How would you define Sabbath?

Why do you think God instituted the Sabbath as part of His Ten Commandments?

....

A few years ago, upon returning from a missions trip, our team stopped in Europe to visit one of our missionaries serving in Ireland. I had never met Holly, yet I'd heard many stories of her sincere love for God and powerful impact as a youth worker throughout Western Europe. As Holly and I became acquainted, she quickly opened up to me about her faith journey. Because of her honesty, it became immediately apparent that Holly was seriously burned-out from life and ministry. It broke my heart to hear of her fragile physical, emotional, and spiritual condition. Within a few months Holly returned to the States and took a medical sabbatical supported by her missions organization. This two-year hiatus involved rest, counseling, and much personal reflection. The Spirit of God led Holly to recalibrate her spiritual journey and calling. Ultimately, she resigned her ministry position and is currently renewing her walk with God and vocational pursuit.

What happened to Holly? How could a godly servant, so in love with the Lord, drift that far? Holly lost center. The imbalanced clay of her life began resisting the directives of the Potter, and the consequences were tragic.

Centering is the act that precedes all others on the potter's wheel. Aligning the clay creates a spinning, un-wobbling pivot so the mud will be free to take innumerable shapes as potter and clay press against each other. If the terra-cotta is not properly centered, it will eventually tear apart, never becoming the vessel the potter desires. Master potter Kristi K. Downing worked with clay for more than 50 years and boldly declared, "Centering is everything."

For the Christian, centering on the potter's wheel is analogous to establishing and maintaining healthy spiritual rhythms. Centering creates a symmetry and harmony in our spiritual lives that sets the stage for the Potter's creative work. Holly lacked margin, rest, balance, and support in core areas of her life and ministry.

·····•·····•··········•···••·········

Read Matthew 11:28–30. What does Jesus promise to those who "come to Him"?

Why is this promise still so significant in twenty-first-century Christianity?

·····•·····•··········•···••·········

Holly is not alone in her experience. Many dedicated followers of Jesus Christ have drifted off-center on the Potter's wheel. Frequently, that drifting takes a dramatic toll on their lives and ministries. Pastor Wayne Cordeiro authored a candid and personal book titled *Leading On Empty*. This honest memoir describes his personal challenges with remaining centered.

> It was a balmy California evening. I had gone for a jog before I was to speak at a leadership conference. I still can't recall how I got there, but I found myself sitting on a curb, weeping uncontrollably. I couldn't tell if it took place suddenly or gradually, but I knew something had broken inside. I remember lifting my trembling hands and asking out loud, "What in the world is happening to me?" I had been leading on empty. That incident on a California curb began a three-year odyssey I never could have imagined. It was a journey through a season of burnout and recalibration that would radically change my lifestyle, my values, my goals, and even readjust my calling.

Staying centered is no easy task for God's people. After reading Pastor Cordeiro's book, reflecting on Holly's story, and reminiscing about my own spiritual journey, I was reminded of three common ways Christians drift off-center on the Potter's wheel.

Unhealthy Boundaries

Staying centered requires we establish healthy limits that enhance the rhythms of life. Boundaries define who we are and what we become. They enrich the property of our lives, like a beautiful Kentucky fence accents the perimeter of a 1,000-acre horse farm. Healthy boundaries push us to take ownership and responsibility for our walks with God, each other, our work, and most importantly ourselves. Establishing physical, mental, emotional, and spiritual boundaries is vital to staying centered on the Potter's wheel.

Workaholism plagued Holly for many years. Some of you reading this chapter are workaholics. Your life is wrapped up in your employment. Holly told me that for a long period of time, she'd never had a weekend off from ministry. Can you imagine the pain of such a demanding and rigorous schedule? According to research by Adrian Gostick and Chester Elton in their book *The Carrot Principle*:

> **Over absorption in one's job often leads to problematic physical and mental health issues. It also threatens marriages, families, and relationships, and can even weaken communities, as employees have less time to volunteer and mentor.**

Now, you and I can sit back and rationalize, saying, "Hey, I work my 40 to 45 hours a week, and then I go home." Yes, maybe, but how many of us are on call 24 hours a day and seven days a week? You may be away from the office, but while at home, you're obsessively checking emails or listening to voice mails. But, of course, you only respond to the "urgent ones." Bob Russell wisely suggested in his sermon, "Balancing Your Schedule," that "Workaholism is the most respectable of all addictions. But if you don't learn to break that habit, it'll one day break you."

••

Read the following passages of Scripture, and describe how Jesus established healthy boundaries in life and ministry.

Mark 1:35

Luke 5:16

Luke 6:12–13

How does spending time alone with God help us establish healthy boundaries?

Are you currently practicing a regular quiet time?

••

Day 2
Unhealthy Grieving

Have you discovered the older you get, the more losses you experience? Recently, a colleague in his early fifties, with whom I had gone to Bible school, got cancer and died within a few months. That is a huge loss for family and friends, disrupting the normal rhythms of life. Holly, the missionary I introduced to you yesterday who suffered from ministry burnout, revealed that between the spring of 2009 and the fall of 2010, she experienced nine traumatic events in her life. These experiences paralyzed her both physically and emotionally. Sadly, she did not know how to deal with them or where to turn.

Holly is not an anomaly. Life is filled with shattered dreams, broken relationships, wayward children, economic woes, health issues, and what the Apostle James labeled as "trials of many kinds" (James 1:2). However, life in the fast lane compounds these sorrows, pushing us to neglect our need to reflect and grieve during times of loss and pain.

A number of years ago a friend lost his wife to cancer. At the memorial service, this gentle and kindhearted man got up and told our church family, "I'm here for you." I lovingly took him aside and shared that although I appreciated his heart, he needed his family and friends to be there for him. Sadly, he did not take my advice and hit the wall. Grief overwhelmed him and, spiritually speaking, tackled him for great losses. He got way off-center on the Potter's wheel, to his own personal hurt and that of his children who needed him most.

••

Write out Matthew 5:4.

According to Psalm 34:18 and Psalm 147:3—how can an individual experience God's blessing even while mourning?

Reflect on a time when you were broken before the Lord. How did you experience God's healing presence in your life?

••

Staying centered demands we learn how to grieve our losses. Time, reflection, and solitude while leaning on God and others—all are

Friendship Church
Prior Lake Campus
October 2, 2016

Pastor Mike Golay
@MikeGolay
#LivingClay

Centered: Are You Too Restless to Rest?

Bob Pierce - if you don't break habitfully break ya! Exodus 20:8-11

Staying Centered: Three Boundaries

- Boundaries at __work__ !   Colossians 3:23-24
  it can be addictive

- Boundaries during __Suffering__ !   Psalm 147:3
  Matt 5:4

- Boundaries of __humility__ !   Proverbs 29:23

The Rest of God - Mark Buchanan

High Capacity personality

The Blessing:

Role model example
should be example

Because the Master Potter gave the Sabbath as a
__gift__ each one of us should embrace the
principle of Sabbath keeping.

Ex 20:8-11

Mark 2:27

G#1. Centered through __Refreshment__ .   Exodus 31:16-17

The Hebrew word **nāpaš** means __Refreshed__

   "taking a deep breath and purposing to refresh oneself"

G#2. Centered through __Worship__ .   Leviticus 23:3

God, you have made us for yourself, and our hearts are restless
till they find their rest in you.

~Augustine

Making It Personal: A Spiritual Inventory

1. Hebrews 11 reminds us that it will take **effort** to enter God's rest.

2. Please take some time to examine your spiritual journey considering the following key areas of life:

    a. Family

    b. Work

    c. Worship (personal and corporate)

    d. Ministry

    e. Social

    f. Physical

3. What areas are currently balanced and healthy?

4. What areas of life seem out of balance and need attention?

Three of the seven books in the Boundary Series
by Dr. Henry Cloud & Dr. John Townsend

essential to the grieving process. Engaging in support ministries such as Grief Share, DivorceCare, Stephen Ministries, or small group fellowships is wise and can provide a safe place for renewal. We need to give ourselves permission to grieve and to experience God's healing touch.

Unhealthy Pride

....

Write out Proverbs 8:13.

How would you define pride? Read the following passages and describe why God hates pride.

Psalm 10:4

Proverbs 13:10

Proverbs 16:18

Daniel 5:17–21

Obadiah 1:3–4

Write out Proverbs 29:23.

What is God's antidote for pride?

....

In *The Rest of God*, Mark Buchanan confesses his obsession with doing more: "I once went 40 days—an ominously biblical number, that—without taking a single day off. And I was proud of it." Many of God's servants replace "being" with "doing" and adopt an egotistical ministry ethic. The preoccupation of busyness can foster an idolatry of self-importance and personal significance. In my early years of ministry, I mistakenly embraced the concept that it is better to wear out than to rust out.

In *Sabbath*, Dan Allender hits this narcissistic nail on the head:

> **Boasting about work is a national pastime. The one who works harder, against greater odds, and with fewer resources to gain the greatest ground wins.**

In his book *The Ten Commandments from the Back Side*, J. Ellsworth Kalas, insightful servant of God, sums up the peril of pride, suggesting, "In some cases our unwillingness to take a Sabbath is evidence of our feeling indispensable—the universe may survive God's taking a day of rest, but it will fall apart if we do so!" Could it be that we arrogantly dishonor the "work-rest cycle," believing that rest means somehow things will not get done, and people are counting on us to do it?

Today, I'm happy to say that I have neither worn out nor rusted out, but rather I have embraced the metaphor that the race of Christianity is more like a marathon than a sprint. Going the distance and finishing well demands proper rest, strategic pacing, and allowing our "doing" to flow from our "being."

••••••••••••••••••••••••••••••••••••••

Read 2 Chronicles 14:1–2. How does Scripture describe King Asa at the beginning of his reign?

Read 2 Chronicles 16:1–12 and answer the following questions.

In the 36th year of Asa's reign, who came against the people of Judah?

How did King Asa respond and who did he seek help from?

In verses 7–9, why did Hanani the Seer rebuke Asa?

How did Asa respond to Hanani?

What happened to King Asa in the final years of his reign?

How does Asa's life illustrate Proverbs 18:12?

••••••••••••••••••••••••••••••••••••••

When we arrogantly think that life and ministry are more about doing than being, we drift off-center and need to repent of such ignorance. Our Creator designed us to live with healthy limits that properly define our humanity. These sacred boundaries are called self-care and involve the pursuit of spiritual, physical, mental, and emotional health. As Parker Palmer states in his book, *Let Your Life Speak: Listening for the Voice of Vocation*, please understand that caring for oneself "is never a selfish act—it is simply good stewardship of the only gift I have, the gift I was put on earth to offer to others."

Day 3
Staying Centered

How do we stay centered on the Potter's wheel? From the beginning of creation, the Master Potter designed His children to live humbly with defined boundaries that include: margins, balance, and healthy spiritual rhythms. More than 3,000 years ago God presented a time-tested way to stay aligned on the Potter's wheel.

••

Read Exodus 20:8–11, and answer the following questions.

Why do you think God rested on the seventh day?

What does it mean that the Lord blessed the Sabbath day and made it holy?

Read Deuteronomy 5:12–15. What reason does God give to Israel for establishing the Sabbath Day?

After 400 years of bondage and unrelenting seven-day workweeks filled with the constant pressure to meet an Egyptian quota, why should this command be viewed as necessary and as a gift?

Why would this Sabbath command require a complete change of mindset to obey?

••

I find it striking that when God gave the Ten Commandments, He had more to say about healthy spiritual rhythms and rest than He did about murder, adultery, or honoring His holy name. However, the commandment of rest is probably the most misunderstood of God's top ten. For many Jews in the ancient world, the Old Testament (OT) was not specific enough regarding the Sabbath imperative so they began making a list on how to or how not to obey this command. In *The Ten Commandments from the Backside*, Kalas desribes:

> By Jesus' time, there were 1,521 things that a person could not do on the Sabbath. The Jerusalem Talmud (Commentary on the OT) had 64 pages [of restrictions] and the Babylonian Talmud 156 double pages of specific rules dealing with the Sabbath. It isn't surprising that many of them took on the quality of the absurd.

For instance, the Sabbath command did not prescribe how far you could travel from your home. Therefore, the Jews determined it was 1,000 yards, which became known as a "Sabbath day's journey" (Acts 1:12). If you tied a knot, you broke the Sabbath. A scribe could not even carry a pen, and a person could not kill a flea or mosquito on the Sabbath, because that constituted effort. A woman could not look in a mirror on the Sabbath, for she might see a gray hair and pull it out. That would be "reaping on the Sabbath day." What God intended as a blessing, to keep our lives centered, ultimately man morphed into a burden. Because of these restrictions, the Sabbath became impossible to live out in a beautiful, God-honoring, and rhythmic manner.

······································

Write out Mark 2:27.

How does this verse support the fact that the Sabbath was given as a blessing and not a burden?

Have you ever seen the Sabbath principle taken in a legalistic or burdensome way? If so, describe the situation and how it impacted your perspective on God's gift of Sabbath.

······································

As the New Testament opens, the reader immediately senses tension around keeping the Sabbath day holy. Jesus engages the controversy head-on, purposing to liberate His followers from the dutiful adherence to Sabbath legalism. The four Gospels record six confrontations between Christ and Jewish religious leaders over Sabbath observances. Five involved healing on the Sabbath, and one incident involved picking heads of grain on the day of rest (Mark 2:23–26). Each time, the Pharisees confront Jesus for violating the Law of Moses as their tradition defined it.

But Jesus defends His actions by pointing out that any Pharisee would rescue an animal that had fallen in a well on the Sabbath day (Luke 14:5). Christ teaches that human need overrules ritual because "the Sabbath was made for man, not man for the Sabbath" (Mark 2:27).

In all six Sabbath confrontations, Jesus does not question the principle of a day of rest. He does, however, bring clarity by teaching and modeling the right use of the day for the people of God. According to the New Testament, Christians are free from a legal approach to keeping the Old Testament Sabbath:

> Therefore do not let anyone judge you by what you eat or drink, or with regard to a religious festival, a New Moon celebration or a Sabbath day. These are a shadow of the things that were to come; the reality, however, is found in Christ. —Colossians 2:16–17

In this passage, Paul provides clarity regarding the religious laws of the Old Covenant, which were a shadow of the substance to come. These regulations were a type of the archetype—Jesus Christ. At Calvary, Jesus established a new religious covenant and therefore, according to Paul, nails the old to the Cross. Staying centered on the Potter's wheel demands that we learn how to enjoy our Sabbath rest, in Christ.

one family's story

When our children were young, our family made a decision to take Sunday and set it apart as holy to the Lord. We chose to slow down by not doing chores or going shopping, but rather to engage our family in events that would bring us together in a special way. Our Sunday Sabbath started with worship then progressed throughout the day with rest, play, and celebrating the gifts of God we experienced throughout the week.

At first our children struggled to embrace our family Sabbath because they wanted to hang out with their friends. In addition, the lawn needed mowing, household chores were not finished, and shopping always seemed necessary.

However, once we began to experience rest and enjoy the Sunday Sabbath, everything changed. Our whole family began looking forward to the life giving dynamics Sunday now afforded.

Recently, our oldest son, who is now 32 years of age, thanked us for establishing the valuable tradition of a day of rest, noting that it is still his "best day of the week."

—Tim and Sharon Whitmore

Day 4
Centered through Rest

Sabbath means "day of rest." The second chapter of Genesis says,

> Thus the heavens and the earth were completed in all their vast array. By the seventh day God had finished the work he had been doing; so on the seventh day he rested from all his work. Then God blessed the seventh day and made it holy, because on it he rested from all the work of creating that he had done. —vv. 1–3

The dominant theme of this passage is the value God places on rest. The principle of Sabbath is so important that God uses Himself as an example.

....

Read Exodus 31:16–17.

Moses states that after God created the heavens and the earth He "rested and was refreshed." The word "refreshed" is *nāpaš* and means taking a deep breath and purposing to refresh oneself. So Sabbath keeping is about breathing and refreshment. List a few ways that celebrating the Sabbath leads to refreshment in our lives.

....

It should be obvious that God chose rest on the seventh day of creation, not because of weariness or exhaustion but out of joy and fulfillment of the work just completed. God establishes a model for healthy rhythms as we celebrate the accomplishments of life, work, and ministry from the previous week. The Sabbath never suggests our work is complete. It does provide, however, a weekly reminder of divine providence and blessing on our lives as we purpose to steward His creation.

....

Reflect on the past week and identify how you have seen God's blessing in the following areas of life.

At home?

At work?

In ministry?

In general?

•••••••••••••••••••••••••••••••••••••

Always remember that the Almighty God, who never fatigues, rested on the seventh day. Therefore, how much more so should His children find rest from their weariness (Isaiah 40:31). As Gordon MacDonald states in *Ordering Your Private World*, "We do not rest because our work is done; we rest because God commanded it and created us to have a need for it." The Apostle Paul makes it clear that believers today are not bound to keep the Sabbath day (Romans 14:1–23; Colossians 2:16–17). However, the principle of resting one day in seven is wise.

One practical purpose for Sabbath-keeping is to create healthy life rhythms and prevent burnout. The testimonies of both Holly and Pastor Wayne Cordeiro illustrate that truth. A few months after Pastor Wayne hit the wall, he learned that individuals who constantly give out wear out because they deplete their bodies' serotonin. This was a new concept for him, and it demanded clarity. He realized that after 30 years of running hard he was leading on empty, and his vocation and future were at stake. Upon returning to his home in Hawaii, he met with Christian psychologist Dr. Archibald Hart who diagnosed him with adrenaline addiction. Dr. Hart explained:

> **Serotonin is a chemical like an endorphin. It's a natural, feel-good hormone. It replenishes during times of rest and then fuels you while you're working. If, however, you continue to drive yourself without replenishing, your store of serotonin will be depleted. As a substitute, your body will be forced to replace the serotonin with adrenaline.**

That revelation became the game changer for God's servant. When he inquired how long it would take to recharge, Dr. Hart told him six months to a year, because his body needed a trickle charge. In the end it took three years to heal completely from leading on empty.

This problem of burnout is not limited to vocational ministers. Anyone can experience adrenaline arousal and deplete his or her serotonin levels when living at breakneck speed. "Type A" personalities are more prone to this condition because of their inherent drive to perform and succeed. Interestingly, a survey in *Inc.* magazine determined that 62 percent of people in America say they feel burned out. You and I can get so many irons in the fire that we put the fire out. The syndrome of burnout is subtle and develops gradually over time. Gary L. McIntosh and Robert L. Edmondson define this malady in *It Only Hurts on Monday* as "the exhaustion of physical, emotional, mental, and spiritual strength or motivation usually caused by prolonged stress or frustration *and inability to appropriate the full spiritual resources of God.*"

From the beginning of creation God established a rhythm for physical, mental, emotional, and spiritual renewal. God's rest is the antidote to burnout from the fast-paced, stress-filled world in which we live. The Sabbath principle suggests that you should cease the strenuous routine of whatever "skilled labor" you are involved in one day a week to enjoy restful delight in God. That may mean leaving your briefcase at the office or bypassing the unfinished chores around the house. We think we get more done by working harder and longer. However, efficiency experts have discovered that reasonably spaced periods of rest increase productivity. Interestingly, starting pitchers in Major League Baseball are given on average four to five days of rest between starts. Baseball professionals know the human arm can only take so much stress before it gives out. The old proverb is true. If you keep your bow bent, it will break.

Doing less is easier said than done. Hard-charging individuals with goal-oriented and time-conscious personalities struggle to take breaks from work. However, valuing our Sabbath rest in Christ frees us from feelings of guilt. Jesus honored the Sabbath and lived perfectly centered. Nobody accomplished more than He did in His three and a half years of public ministry. How about taking a few moments to examine your spiritual journey by answering the following questions?

Are you running at breakneck speed?

If yes, what is pushing you so hard?

Does your spiritual GPS need recalibrating?

If yes, what might that look like?

Have you ever considered that you might be too restless to rest?

Is it possible that you value *doing* more than you value *being* and living with healthy, rest-filled, spiritual rhythms?

Do you ever struggle with feelings of guilt when you take time off for rest and renewal?

Day 5
Centered through Worship

G od told Moses, "Remember the Sabbath day by keeping it holy" (Exodus 20:8). Then He reminded his servant, saying, "Therefore the LORD blessed the Sabbath day and made it holy" (Exodus 20:11). The Hebrew word for "holy" is qādaš, and it means, "to consecrate, sanctify, or dedicate." According to Dan Allender in his book, *Sabbath*, "Jewish people refer to the Sabbath as the 'queen.' The word *sanctify* has the meaning of betrothal." This implies that Sabbath-keeping is a holy union between God's people—as lovers enjoy sacred time together. Staying centered in worship suggests we prioritize and consecrate one day a week for the Lord. Our "Christian Sabbath" should involve a change of pace and plan that is unique, reserved as special and holy unto the Lord. In his book, *Margin*, Richard Swenson suggests: "At Sabbath time we suspend dominion work and instead worship the dominion-Maker. We cease reaping for our own cupboards and instead bring an offering to Him."

••••••••••••••••••••••••••••••••

Read Leviticus 23:3. Why do you think God called the Sabbath a "day of sacred assembly"?

••••••••••••••••••••••••••••••••

Moses wants us to know that in addition to rest, the Sabbath day involves gathering for worship. This sacred assembly is an outward and communal expression of an inward and ongoing attitude, of perpetual devotion in our hearts. Sacred times for worship assist God's people in staying centered in their faith. Slowing down to reflect and celebrate His goodness fulfills the command of God's community, offering a sacrifice of praise (Hebrews 13:15).

The Masoretic Text of the Old Testament designates Psalm 92 for use on the Sabbath day. It is the only Psalm with this heading. We can learn much about centering our lives from this beautiful hymn of praise. For instance, spiritual alignment involves praising Yahweh for His loyal love and faithfulness (vv. 2–4), celebrating the greatness of His works in our lives (vv. 5–7), and having as the ultimate goal of life the exaltation of His glorious name (v. 8). These guidelines for honoring the sacred assembly put our attention on God, resulting in a peaceful perspective on the cares, pressures, and pursuits of the world.

••••••••••••••••••••••••••••••••••••

Read Luke 4:16 and describe how Jesus lived a completely balanced life by prioritizing worship and faith renewal on the Sabbath day.

Why do you think Luke put such an emphasis on the spiritual routine of Jesus that involved corporate worship on the Sabbath day?

••••••••••••••••••••••••••••••••••••

Because of the Resurrection of Jesus Christ from the grave, the New Testament introduces the Lord's Day as the special day of worship for Christians (Acts 20:7; 1 Corinthians 16:1–4; Revelation 1:9–10). Although some have made the Lord's Day their Sabbath, the Bible makes it clear that every day is holy unto the Lord (Colossians 2:16–23; Romans 14:5–23). Therefore, the people of God have greater flexibility to choose a day of distinction, beginning with the Lord's Day, in order to stay centered through worship. Worship promotes centering one's life on God, who is the same yesterday, today, and forever (Hebrews 13:8). In worship, we experience a fixed center of reality, including the eternal Word of God (Isaiah 40:8) and Jesus Christ, the eternal and unchangeable Son of God (John 1:1–4).

Sadly, today many in our culture neglect corporate worship. According to Rebecca Barnes and Lindy Lowry's study on church attendance in America, an estimated 78 million Protestants attend church less than 12 times a year and inactive church members range between 40 to 60 percent of the actual congregation's membership. I am convinced that there is a direct link between a lack of worship and our fast-paced, stress-filled, burned-out culture. Genuine worship, done in spirit and truth, prevents the clay of our lives from getting off-center and becoming unstable—also preventing destructive outcomes.

••••••••••••••••••••••••••••••••••••

Write out Hebrews 10:24–25.

What is the primary concern in this passage as it relates to worship?

Have you ever neglected corporate worship?

If yes, how did that impact your walk with the Lord?

••

A. W. Tozer suggests:

> Worship is the missing jewel in modern evangelicalism. We're organized; we work; we have our agendas. We have almost everything, but there's one thing that the churches, even the gospel churches, do not have: that is the ability to worship. We are not cultivating the art of worship. It's the one shining gem that is lost to the modern church, and I believe that we ought to search for this until we find it.

Experiencing spiritual rest in corporate worship is only a shadow of the substance of God's grander scheme. I have congregants regularly tell me that Sunday morning worship is their favorite time of the week. With great anticipation, these individuals look forward to experiencing the presence and power of God in corporate gatherings. As they give to God in worship, they also receive the blessing of spiritual renewal. They gain strength from God and one another, which prepares them for the week to come.

Pastor Wayne Cordeiro further shared, in *Leading on Empty* how his psychologist Archibald Hart suggested, "Your soul is like a battery that discharges each time you give life away, and it needs to be recharged regularly."

We must remember that the physical rest of Exodus 20:8–11 anticipated the new covenant and eternal heavenly rest. The writer to the Hebrews paints a wonderful portrait of this heavenly rest:

> There remains, then, a Sabbath-rest for the people of God; for anyone who enters God's rest also rests from his own works, just as God did from his. Let us, therefore, make every effort to enter that rest, so that no one will perish by following their example of disobedience. —Hebrews 4:9–11

This passage describes repose of the heart as the by-product of our worship and love relationship with Jesus Christ. Hebrews reminds us that it will take an effort to enter into this type of rest. Paradoxically, the prerequisite for rest is work. Entering God's rest and experiencing His best takes spiritual energy. This effort to experience a break suggests that the gift of Sabbath-rest must be prioritized in our schedules. Recently our church approved a sabbatical policy for the pastoral staff. This past summer, a member of our leadership team enjoyed a ten-week breather from the rigors and demands of ministry. He told me that the sabbatical may have saved his ministry. But pulling off an intentional sabbatical takes effort. It has to be detailed, properly communicated, and embraced by the congregation. It demands proactive planning, creativity, and discernment by the pastoral family and church body in order for the work-rest motif to transpire. Make it a priority, it's worth the work.

Jesus invited us to experience this rest when He said:

Come to me, all you who are weary and burdened, and I will give you rest. Take my yoke upon you and learn from me, for I am gentle and humble in heart, and you will find rest for your souls. For my yoke is easy and my burden is light. —Matthew 11:28–30

Back during the 1980s, before voice mail was built right into cell phones, people used to get units called "answering machines" that ran on four batteries and used tape recorders that could be rewound to hear messages. The power these machines used up by being "on" all day and night quickly drained the batteries. So, one company invented a self-charging battery. This battery cost a bit more initially, but when it ran out of power it could be pulled from the machine, set aside, and recharged. All it needed was adequate rest and a chance to revitalize its drained capacity. Many Christians are the same way. They need a chance to pull back, rest, and recharge now and then.

May I encourage you to accept the invitation of the Savior? Prioritize the sacred assembly as a place to experience God and find rest. Spend time in prayer, asking God to help you understand how to enjoy His rest. Get creative, and experiment with different routines. There are no perfect formulas in pursuing healthy spiritual rhythms. Grow to value seasons of silence, solitude, and scriptural meditation. Learn to relax at the feet of Jesus. Discipline yourself by establishing specific times each day to recalibrate your walk with Christ. View your day as a spiritual journey with dedicated rest stops along the way. Get innovative at work or at home, and have fun redeeming time for the Lord. Why not take a morning or afternoon break a few times a week for Scripture reading or a prayerwalk? How about fasting a meal or two each week and dedicating that time to reading a book or memorizing a passage of Scripture? Give the TV, computer, or social media a few evenings off, and spend time seeking God alone or with your family. Read the classic works written on soul care (see the recommended resources section for a list of such titles), and nurture your practice of the presence of God. These habits of the heart provide the environment for you to meet with the Good Shepherd. He longs for you to experience green pastures and quiet waters that ultimately restore your soul (Psalm 23:1–3).

Day 6
Too Restless to Rest

During the past 30 years, God has called me to serve as the lead pastor in two turnaround ministry settings. Much of my vocational ministry has been dedicated to triage and healing of very fragile spiritual environments. I'm thankful for the opportunities to serve in this capacity. A few years ago, I knew something was wrong but, like Wayne Cordeiro, I could not put my finger on the problem. Providentially, I was introduced to the ministry of SonScape Retreats located near Colorado Springs, Colorado. My wife and I attended a weeklong getaway that launched our journey of renewal.

SonScape became a safe place to tell our story. We found encouragement, blessing, and counseling fitted to our unique situation. The leadership strategically designed the retreat around worship, rest, as well as group and individual counseling. During that week my wife and I experienced God in a new and living way. Refreshment came through sacred assembly, quiet time, prayerwalks, and enjoyment of God's creation. We slept in, learned to relax again, and even enjoyed the comfort of a hot tub off our back porch while viewing Pike's Peak. We returned from SonScape renewed and with a greater passion to create healthy spiritual rhythms for our church staff, our family, and ourselves. As lead pastor, I am convinced this is one of the best gifts I can give my colleagues in ministry.

I want to encourage you not to wait until a crisis hits before practicing the Christian Sabbath. Mark Buchanan wrote in *The Rest of God* that he "learned to keep Sabbath in the crucible of breaking it" for more than 20 years. However, it was neither Scripture nor the Spirit's conviction that got his attention but rather his unraveling life and ministry. He candidly summarizes his story:

> **Plain and simple, I was worn out. I knew that if I didn't recover the art of rest—if I failed to find the rest of God—I would watch all my works and all my days turn to blight. I became . . . a Sabbath-keeper the hard way.**

The Potter welcomes us to live centered on His wheel by entering His rest. Will you accept the invitation to physical, emotional, mental, and spiritual rhythms of life? Will you make the sacred assembly a priority in your worship week? Will you live on center and find rest for your soul?

Father,
I confess that staying centered on the wheel is hard work.
Please reveal to me where I am not centered. I long to live with healthy boundaries but need Your wisdom and discernment to establish them. Help me to create structures that are unique to Your calling on my life. Forgive me, Lord, when doing trumps being. Let my doing always flow out of my being. I long to worship You in spirit and truth. Thank You for providing rest for my soul. In Jesus' name, I pray.
Amen.

spiritual inventory

Hebrews 4:11 reminds us that it will take effort to enter God's rest. Take some time to examine your spiritual journey considering the following key areas of life:

Family_____

Work_____

Worship (personal and corporate)_____

Ministry_____

Social_____

Physical_____

What areas are currently balanced and healthy?_____

_____

What areas of life seem out of balance and need attention?_____

_____

WEEK 4

....

CRUSHING: *The Gift of Crushing*

JOB 10:8–9

*God permits what He hates to accomplish
that which He loves.*

—Joni Eareckson Tada

Day 1
Taming the Clay

I will always remember how I felt and responded when Gregorio, the master potter in Romania, locked his hands together and then, with great precision and force, plastered the clay vessel back to the wheel. *What just happened?* I thought. *The piece being shaped looked really nice. Why are you starting over? Seems like a waste of time and energy!* Then God spoke, "Keith, this is part of the process of My shaping you in to the image of My Son during the past 20 years."

As tears welled in my eyes, the Spirit of God warmed my heart with awe and appreciation for the Master Potter's care. However, that moment also opened a floodgate of questions regarding how the Potter interacts with the clay: *Why God, do You have to smash us down on Your wheel again? In Your crushing, will You create something better, purer, and more lasting? Lord, You know Your strong hands hurt, right? Is it really necessary?*

Pressing the clay downward on the wheel is called "taming the clay," which prevents any tendencies the clay might have to behave erratically. Potters view the clay as alive in their hands. Taming the clay is the Potter's way of letting the clay know that the hands of the Potter are loving and caring but also sovereign.

As clay in the Potter's hands, we must learn to value God's crushing in our lives. The Book of Job demonstrates that not only will the crushing take place, but at times we will struggle to accept what feels like God's heavy hand in our life.

....

Read Job 10:8–9. What do Job's questions reveal about his feelings toward God's crushing in his life?

....

The Bible makes it clear that God permitted Job's painful experiences (Job 1:8). The Potter put His servant's life on the wheel for purposes initially unknown to Job. Every Christ follower who has journeyed with the Lord for any period of time has shared in Job's experience and dilemma.

....

Consider the following servants of the Lord and how they responded to the Potter's spiritual formation in their life.

Read 1 Samuel 1:1–11. Describe Hannah's painful situation and the agony she felt on the Potter's wheel.

How did Hannah lean into the Potter's crushing (vv. 10–11)?

Read Genesis 32:22–32. Here we see Jacob, the patriarch, wrestling all night with the Lord. What did God choose to do to Jacob in order for him to surrender?

Put yourself in Jacob's shoes. How would you feel if God permanently handicapped your life in a wrestling match?

What might God be purposing to accomplish in Jacob through this encounter?

Read Matthew 16:15–23. The Apostle Peter regularly felt the crushing blow of the Potter's hands. At one point in his faith formation, the Potter's shaping looked great as Peter confessed Jesus Christ as the Messiah. However, that same clay experienced a crushing blow, when the Potter rebuked him.

If you were Peter how would you feel if Jesus used such strong language while mentoring you (v. 23)?

When you look at all these stories together, what conclusions can you make regarding God's crushing blows in our lives?

....

Day 2
Becoming Weak

•••••••••••••••••••••••••••••••••••••••

The Apostle Paul was no stranger to crushing. *Read 2 Corinthians 12:7–10.* What did Paul beg God to remove from his life?

How did God respond?

What value did Paul place on his challenging experiences?

•••••••••••••••••••••••••••••••••••••••

Jesus made it clear that "whoever does not carry their cross and follow me cannot be my disciple" (Luke 14:27). At times, the Cross of Christ involves crushing. Lee Strobel commissioned a Barna survey for his book, *The Case for Faith*, asking thousands of adults, "If you could ask God only one question and you knew He would give you an answer, what would you ask?" The most common question was, "Why is there pain and suffering in the world?"

Whether we call it anguish, crushing, trials, or tribulations, suffering is one of the great equalizers in life. We all encounter it—some more than others. In his book, *Where is God When It Hurts*, Philip Yancey further develops the tension we all feel when he writes:

Christians who believe in a loving Creator, don't really know how to interpret pain. If pinned against the wall at a dark, secret moment, many Christians would confess that pain was God's one mistake. Really, he should have worked a little harder to devise a better way for us to cope with danger.

After a season of "feasting on love," C. S. Lewis lost his dear wife, Joy, to bone cancer in July of 1960. His hallmark book, *A Grief Observed*, describes with great detail the hurt he experienced through that loss. Consider how this saintly man wrestled to reconcile the crushing blow of losing his beloved spouse of only three years to cancer:

Talk to me about the truth of religion and I'll listen gladly. Talk to me about the duty of religion and I'll listen submissively. But don't come talking to me about the consolation of religion or I shall suspect that you don't understand. The conclusion is not, "So there's

no God, after all" but "So this is what God is really like, the Cosmic Sadist. The spiteful imbecile?"

···

Have you ever felt like C. S. Lewis and been deeply hurt by God? How did you deal with that painful situation?

···

Like many of us who have been hurt deeply in life, C. S. Lewis struggled for a season to reconcile God's silence and sovereignty in the midst of pain. History is replete with stories of righteous men and women who questioned God for what they considered injustice and God's poor management of His creation. Think through the Old Testament Book of Psalms for a moment. Forty percent of the 150 songs are categorized as individual or communal laments. Many of these dirges have to do with personal suffering and the perceived absence of God. These cries from the heart remind us that we are what we sing and the soul regularly carries significant sorrow. The people of Israel sang about their painful experiences, perpetual losses, and ongoing struggles. Their hymns purposed to reconcile the hurt that life continually afforded and how God met them in their time of trouble.

Sadly, some devout Christians abort faith because of their inability to reconcile human suffering with a loving and gracious God. Part of our dilemma includes our struggle to trust God and see the big picture. In addition, we periodically confuse our painful experiences as synonymous with evil. We can see them as punishment for evil, which they are not necessarily. Job's friends hammered him with this worldview, resulting in frustration, discouragement, and hurt for Job. Similarly, Jesus' disciples got caught in this theological impasse so they inquired, "Rabbi, who sinned, this man or his parents, that he was born blind?" (John 9:2). The disciples of Christ shared the perspective of Job's colleagues. Without hesitation Jesus reminded his followers that God had a greater purpose for this man's blindness and suffering.

As I edit this chapter, my thoughts turn to a godly friend, in his early sixties, who is in the final stages of cancer. For the past three decades, his testimony has brought glory to God and impacted many people.

However, cancer did not end his impact for Christ but rather multiplied it as his life continues to testify of God's glory and grace.

Jesus embraced the brokenness we all experience when He wept over the death of His friend Lazarus (John 11:35) and cried out for the people of Jerusalem (Matthew 23:37). In Gethsemane He sweated drops of blood (Luke 22:44) and agonized at Calvary when He cried, "My God, my God, why have you forsaken me?" (Matthew 27:46). The writer to the Hebrews summarizes the anguish of the Savior stating that during His lifetime, Jesus "offered up prayers and petitions with fervent cries" (Hebrews 5:7).

The life of Christ demonstrates the truth quadriplegic Joni Eareckson Tada testifies, that God, at times, allows what He hates to accomplish what He loves.

Recently, I experienced an abscessed tooth. The extreme discomfort alerted me to make an appointment immediately to see my dentist. After two hours of surgery that left my head numb for hours, I thanked my doctor and my God for the healing process that began with severe pain. The Word of God demonstrates that the clay can learn to value God's crushing as a gift, regardless of how painful it may feel at the time.

••••••••••••••••••••••••••••••••••••••

Take a moment and reflect on a time when pain and suffering produced spiritual fruit in your life. Describe that situation and the growth that resulted.

••••••••••••••••••••••••••••••••••••••

Day 3
Clarity

D r. Paul Brand coauthored a book with Philip Yancey entitled *The Gift of Pain*, which earned the Gold Medallion Book Award. Dr. Brand grew up as a missionary kid in India, and for more than 20 years, he worked among impoverished leprosy patients. After many years of research, he learned that lepers were living in great danger because of their painlessness. Dr. Brand's pioneering research in India established that in virtually all cases, leprosy numbs the extremities. The result: tissue damage to the hands, feet, nose, ears, eyes, and face because the warning system of pain has fallen silent in the body. Dr. Brand reminds us that God designed our physical bodies to experience pain for our protection. The problem with lepers is that their bodies cannot recognize pain because their pain cells are anesthetized. Leprosy is a disease of the nervous system. That is why Dr. Paul Brand says with utter sincerity, "Thank God for pain!" and concludes, "pain is not the enemy, but the loyal scout announcing the enemy." God built into the body the gift of pain to protect, forewarn, and provide a way of staying healthy. The sensation of pain is a gift—the gift nobody wants. More than anything, pain should be viewed as God's communication network.

May I propose that what is true physically about pain is also true spiritually? Yes, at times, life in the Potter's hands can seem unbearable. But, the Potter's crushing is always purposeful, and we can embrace the painful experience as a gift. James, the brother of Jesus who personally witnessed the Crucifixion of Christ, understood the gift of pain and offers clarity. In his short epistle, he wrote to his kinsmen scattered among the nations and exhorted them to get God's perspective on the trials and sufferings stating,

> **Consider it pure joy, my brothers and sisters, whenever you face trials of many kinds, because you know that the testing of your faith produces perseverance. Let perseverance finish its work so that you may be mature and complete, not lacking anything. —James 1:2–4**

....

Perspective is vital to experience pure joy. According to James, what is God testing and why is that testing important?

What primary attribute does God purpose to develop in the testing?

What grander results does the Potter purpose as we lean into our trials?

....

These first-century Jewish believers knew full well the story of Job. They could identify with how he'd felt on the Potter's wheel and their need to respond in a God-honoring way. While suffering for their faith and fleeing like fugitives throughout the Mediterranean world, these first-century Christ followers were provided hope from James in the midst of pain. His advice transcends time and supports us in responding to the painful trials we all experience on the Potter's wheel.

There are times when life on the Potter's wheel prompts more questions than it answers. You may recall that Job's pain ran so deep he wound up cursing the day he was born (Job 3:1). His wife, on the other hand, defected, and counseled her husband to "curse God and die" (Job 2:9). His best friends struggled to recognize the Potter's wisdom, so they moralized about Job's suffering, suggesting he was receiving his due reward for his sinful lifestyle (Job 4:7–9). How unfortunate that his beloved spouse and close friends offered horrendous counsel. In some ways, they made Job's dilemma much worse.

....

Are you currently experiencing a trial that you need God's perspective on?

Are you persevering in the trial or shrinking back?

James reminds us that we can ask God for wisdom in the midst of trial (James 1:5). Take a moment to pray and talk to God about the trial you are currently experiencing and how He would have you respond.

....

Day 4
Growth

O ne of the most challenging realities you and I will face as clay on the Potter's wheel is submitting to His crushing blows and growing in our faith through them.

•••

Read Matthew 13:20–21. What concern did Jesus express about the tactics of Satan when it comes to persecution and suffering?

Have you ever seen the enemy use pain and suffering to destroy the faith of another?

•••

Without minimizing everything Job experienced, I would propose that James had a much clearer perspective on how to properly respond to the God-ordained trials of life. James wrote, "Consider it pure joy, my brothers and sisters, whenever you face trials of many kinds" (James 1:2). The brother of Jesus addressed life on the Potter's wheel frankly and honestly.

•••

In James 1:2, what does the word "whenever" imply?

•••

This passage reminds us that crushing is not a question of *if* but rather a declaration of *when*. That is why the late preacher Joseph Parker once said, "Preach to the suffering, and you will never lack a congregation. There is a broken heart in every pew." Job's crushing was severe, for in a brief period of time he lost many things all of us deeply value, including his children, his wealth, and his health (Job 1:13–2:8). Now, you and I may never experience the intensity or severity of trials Job did, and for that we should thank God. However, most of us will feel like Job in one or more moments of our lives because we will experience significant loss, pain, and crushing in the Potter's hand. When you least expect it, a loved one may commit suicide, or a spouse may engage in infidelity. Or perhaps a simple checkup with your family physician will result in a diagnosis of cancer and immediate surgery. Maybe you'll find yourself in the final stages of the adoption process, and the mother will decide to keep her child. Or your boss might come to you with the proposition of relocation or losing your job. Friends who once seemed loyal may turn their backs on you, resulting in extreme loneliness and hurt.

James longs for us to submit to the hands of the Potter, so he offers healthy counsel when dealing with the painful trials of life. He reminds us that trouble is not an elective; it is a required course. Years ago, I read an article that professional golfer Bobby Jones wrote for *Golf Magazine* discussing the challenge of sand traps in the game of golf. I can't remember the exact words he used, but he said something like, "It is interesting you hardly ever see players practicing sand shots." I laughed upon hearing that truth because, as a recreational golfer, I too have never practiced getting out of the beach. This kernel of truth stuck out to me. Jones wisely advises golfers with the idea that all players, even the best, wind up in the bunker from time to time. We should acknowledge the crucial role of recovery work, not be surprised when the hard shots come, and prepare ourselves for them as best we can. In golf, as in life, as much as we may work to minimize hardship, we can never avoid all difficult situations. We need to learn how to work our way out of tough spots and build our coping skills.

What great advice, not only for the game of golf but also for life on the Potter's wheel. Just as golfers need to practice sand shots, so we, the clay, need to realize that crushing is an inevitable part of life on the Potter's wheel. Always remember that this divine instruction purposes growth, fruit, and Christlike character. Therefore, lean into His crushing and let the Potter continue to shape a masterpiece.

••

Write out 1 Peter 4:12.

Why do you think Peter addressed the "surprise" factor?

Does this concept suggest that our expectations of life on the Potter's wheel are different than the Potter's expectations?

••

These two great men of faith remind us that crushing comes uniquely because the Potter works with the clay in very personalized ways.

By implication, what you are struggling with may be incredibly different from the next person, and rest assured that some trials bite harder than others. Some of us experience fender benders while others encounter head-on collisions. One person may lose his wallet; another may have the stock market fall out from under him. Someone may suffer a twisted ankle, another a broken bone. One may experience friction at the office, the other the divorce of a loved one. One may be suffering from a migraine headache, the other a brain tumor. Clearly the Potter interacts with every lump of clay dynamically.

Over the years, I have discovered that some people try to give the impression that once you become a Christian, life on the Potter's wheel is absolutely comfortable. That person is either speaking from an empty head or a closed Bible. Like Job, James lived in reality, and he wrote to clarify that trials are an inevitable part of becoming useful to the Potter. That is why A. W. Tozer said, "It is doubtful whether God can bless a man greatly until He has hurt him deeply." Pain produces pliability in the clay. Suffering helps the clay to submit and experience true and lasting transformation. Recently, a friend shared that after losing his job and having his salary significantly decreased, he and his wife have experienced spiritual blessings in ways previously unsurpassed in their journey with Christ. These trials caused them to refocus and reprioritize their lives and grow deeper in their walk with Christ. Although God's ways might not be something we would choose, great comfort comes in the knowledge that His thoughts and ways are higher and therefore best (Isaiah 55:9).

Do you agree with A. W. Tozer? Why or why not?

Read Romans 5:3–5. How does this passage show that these seemingly severe blows from the Master Potter are always motivated by love and strategically planned for our good and for His glory?

Day 5
Purposeful

When the potter smashes the clay on the wheel, he does so purposefully. A flaw may arise in the form of a wobble, crack, or deep gouge. Marred clay cannot become the beautiful bowl, vase, or goblet the potter intends. In addition, there may be times the potter simply decides to start over, having a grander purpose in mind. The real question is: how will the clay react to the purposeful hands of the Potter?

James provides motivation for a God-honoring response to the Potter's purposeful plan.

....

Read James 1:2–4. Why is perseverance such an important attribute in bringing the clay to completion and usefulness?

....

When we welcome adversity as James promotes, our character forms in ways that it could never have without the testing because trials serve to evaluate the quality of the clay and produce the Spirit's fruit of patient endurance. But welcoming hardship is easier said than done. Think about it. When was the last time you prayed for God to test the quality of your faith through trials? Welcoming trials does not mean getting up in the morning and asking God to make life hard. No, embracing hardship means that we will lean into the trials when they come and grow through painful experiences.

Scott Peck, in his intriguing book *The Road Less Traveled*, explains why painful experiences on the Potter's wheel are necessary and should be welcomed:

> It is in this whole process of meeting and solving problems that life has its meaning. Problems are the cutting edge that distinguishes between success and failure. Problems call forth courage and wisdom. . . . It is only because of problems that we grow mentally and spiritually. . . . It is for this reason that wise people learn not to dread but actually to welcome problems.

At age 17, Joni Eareckson Tada crushed her spinal cord while diving in the Chesapeake Bay. After being confined to a wheelchair for over 40 years, Joni continues to wholeheartedly validate the perspective of James.

In her book, *Making Sense of Suffering*, she says, "suffering provides the gym equipment on which [her] faith can be exercised." How encouraging to know that in the midst of trials, the clay need not inquire about the why behind the crushing. Rather, the clay seeks to discern what spiritual attributes the Potter is intending to form in the clay. The ultimate goal of the Christian life has never been our comfort but rather the development of Christlike character. Now, I am not suggesting that Scripture requires that we find a silver lining in every aspect of our suffering. Our painful trials are more complex than that, especially when, like Job, we lose everything (Job 1–2). However, we must think biblically so we don't misrepresent the Potter's purposeful crushing, like Job's colleagues did, and wrongly circle the wagons of despair. It brought the Apostle Paul great joy when he witnessed God's people growing in the midst of painful trials—and that is the Potter's vision for every hardship we experience.

....

Read 2 Thessalonians 1:3–4. Why did Paul commend the Thessalonian church?

Take a moment and list three to four individuals who are models of perseverance in the faith.

How does their example encourage you to "press on" to win the prize for which God has called you in Christ Jesus?

Similarly, the Apostle Peter sees great value in trials because they prove our faith genuine. According to 1 Peter 1:6–7 what do our trials prove and ultimately result in?

....

Job progressively saw the spiritual purpose and value of life on the Potter's wheel when he concluded, "But he knows the way that I take; when he has tested me, I will come forth as gold" (Job 23:10). The great Puritan Samuel Rutherford captured the value of suffering when he stated, "When I am in the cellar of affliction, I look for the Lord's choicest wines." Pain and hardship can actually draw us closer to our Savior, for we are privileged to share in the sufferings of Christ (1 Peter 4:13; Philippians 3:10). In pastoral ministry, I periodically hear believers say, "I would never have wished that painful experience on anyone, but I would certainly not trade that encounter with God for the world."

In my own faith journey, God has used suffering to break through certain strongholds that marred the clay of my life. A number of years ago, our family was living and pastoring in Southwest Virginia. In a brief period of time, I was diagnosed with three significant, painful, and debilitating ailments: iritis, peritonsillar abscess, and carotidynia. Not familiar with these conditions? Neither was I. In fact, all three of the doctors who treated me seemed somewhat surprised that I was dealing with all of these infirmities. These incapacitating diseases seemed to be the result of stress caused by the pressures of pastoral ministry. Although I felt spiritually strong, my physical body was telling me just the opposite. The pressures of a turn-around ministry context mushroomed to the point where my body broke down and said, no more, this hurts too much.

Looking back, I would never wish those ailments and painful experiences on anyone; however, today I am convinced they resulted in personal and pastoral maturity. Through these trials I matured as a believer and in my ability to shepherd the flock of God. I believe the pain is always worth the freedom and maturity that results.

........•........•........•........•..........

How about you? Do you welcome the painful process of crushing?

Do you see the spiritual value like James, Peter, and Paul did?

When you look back on suffering, do you embrace God's growth plan, and can you say today that it was worthwhile?

Will you hold fast to the truth that God is more interested in shaping your character than providing your comfort?

Next time you feel His crushing blow—will you choose joy in the midst of pain?

........•........•........•........•..........

Day 6
Blessing

R adio personality Paul Harvey made famous the tagline, "Now the rest of the story." Chapter 42 of Job wraps up the book of crushing. This climactic ending describes God's multiplied blessing on Job's life, because he endured the painful work of the Potter.

••••••••••••••••••••••••••••••••••••••

Read Job 42:12–17. Why do you think the Potter blessed Job's life greater in the end?

Describe the unique blessings he received from the Lord.

••••••••••••••••••••••••••••••••••••••

In addition to these many gifts from God, Job reflected on his greatest blessing: a deeper relationship with his Lord. The great patriarch declared, "My ears had heard of you but now my eyes have seen you" (Job 42:5). Therefore, God's benevolence included both physical and spiritual rewards.

James wanted us to know that crushing and blessing exist in tandem and can provide hope in the midst of suffering: "Blessed is the one who perseveres under trial because, having stood the test, that person will receive the crown of life that the Lord has promised to those who love him" (James 1:12). This crown of life is best translated, "the crown that is life." James is motivational and encourages his readers to remember that eternal life is the ultimate reward for perseverance and faithfulness but that God will indeed meet us with blessing at our point of need even here on earth.

Now we must ask the question, "Who is this person the Bible calls blessed?" Jesus describes this individual as one who finds complete satisfaction in God, regardless of his or her situation. According to Christ, that person may be brokenhearted, humble, hungry, or persecuted but nonetheless very happy (Matthew 5:1–12). From a worldly point of view, this perspective seems like a contradiction, but the Master Potter has a grander scheme in mind than anything the world can offer.

James highlighted one particular "beatitude" describing God's blessing by borrowing the word "crown" from the athletic world. When victorious, ancient athletes were crowned with garland wreaths to symbolize persevering triumph. The Apostle Paul reminds us that running the race is hard; however, reward follows for those who run faithfully (1 Corinthians 9:24–27). It appears that the phrase "the crown of life" was a well-known idiom in the first century, as illustrated by the Apostle John's use of it in Revelation 2:10. According to John Brown's *Lectures on the Book of Revelation*, Archbishop Trench says the crown of life is "the emblem not of royalty, but of highest joy and gladness, of glory and immortality." The phrase suggests a quality of life that could not be experienced outside the Potter's crushing blows. God uses trials as a necessary part of spiritual formation. He hurts us to help us become more like His Son.

Professional surfer Bethany Hamilton demonstrates how an individual can experience clarity, spiritual growth, and God's blessing even during times of great crushing. At age eight, Bethany began competing as a surfer in Hawaii. By age 13, she had won numerous surfing competitions. On October 31, 2003, Bethany and a few friends, were enjoying an early morning surf along Tunnels Beach, off the northern Hawaiian island of Kauai. While Bethany was lying sideways on her surfboard with her left arm hanging in the water, a 14-foot tiger shark attacked her, severing her left arm just below the shoulder. Without delay, her friends got her to Wilcox Memorial Hospital. As loved ones gathered at the hospital and prayed, Bethany's parents joyfully reported that their daughter was going to live. Further, Bethany immediately wanted her family and friends to know that "she thanked God that this happened to her so she can tell everyone about Jesus." How remarkable for a teenager to have such clarity of purpose while encountering such loss.

Bethany's mom, Cheri, quickly recognized the Potter's work. Cheri described how she and Bethany had recently been praying that the Lord would make Bethany's life count for Christ in a significant way. The Master Potter answered that bold prayer. Since the tragedy, her walk with Christ has matured well beyond her years. This crushing blow has resulted in significant ministry opportunities and unexpected blessings. In 2004, her book, *Soul Surfer: A True Story of Faith, Family, and Fighting to Get Back on the Board*, was published. By 2010 it had sold more than 1.5 million copies. A year later, she traveled to Germany to support United States troops who lost limbs in combat. God has provided one platform after another to share her story and the good news of Jesus Christ. In 2011, Anna Sophia Robb portrayed her in the film *Soul Surfer*. In a biography written by Tom Price, Bethany summarizes her painful experience with the Master Potter:

> God has definitely answered my prayer to use me. He speaks to people when they hear my story—whether they read one of my books, watched my documentary, or saw me in person, on TV, in a magazine, or a newspaper. People tell me that they have drawn closer to God, started to believe in God, found hope for their lives, or were inspired to overcome a difficult circumstance. I just praise God when I hear those things because it's not me doing anything for them— God is the One Who is helping them. I'm so stoked that God would let me be a part of His plan.

As difficult as this may be to hear, the Master Potter knows what He is doing. Job's life clearly illustrates that truth. Since the Potter has our best in mind, James challenges us to be joyful and persevere in the midst of suffering. The ongoing crushing is designed to reshape you, not ruin you. Yes, crushing is a gift from God, but it is a gift no one wants.

••

Given what God has taught you in this chapter on crushing, how do you hope to respond the next time you feel flattened on the Potter's wheel?

At the most macro level, will you choose, like Bethany Hamilton, to embrace the Potter's smashing with spiritual clarity, growth, purpose, and blessing?

••

Father,
I have to be honest: suffering is hard for me, and I often
want to jump off Your wheel. But, today, I choose to embrace a new
perspective—that Your crushing has value and should be viewed as a
gift. Help me to grow to know You better, like Job did. Give me
courage to embrace these truths James and Peter taught. Thank You,
Father, for Your strong but tender hands. Thank You for shaping
me through pain and suffering. In Jesus' name, I pray.
Amen.

WEEK 5

GRACE: *Let God's Grace Amaze You*

JEREMIAH 18

*The law tells me how crooked I am; grace
comes along and straightens me out.
—Dwight L. Moody*

Day 1
Contaminated

D ozens of students did their best to follow their teacher's instructions. They centered and shaped the clay. Each one crafted his
or her piece uniquely. No two pieces were alike. The young
potters' fingerprints were all over these works of art. Each pupil lined
up to place his or her piece in the kiln for firing. Anticipation filled the
air. As the temperature increased, so did expectation and excitement.
What would their pieces look like? Would the glazes bring forth the
color complement they hoped for? Would their art teacher, Lucas Magnuson, be pleased? Would they receive a good grade? But when the
instructor opened the kiln, the students' countenances fell. The guts of
the kiln looked like a war zone. The vast majority of pieces had exploded
during the firing process. That occurrence became a teachable moment
for everyone. Even the art teacher had never seen a disaster like this
one. What had gone wrong? What had caused virtually every piece in
the kiln to shatter? Lucas had only one answer: contaminated clay.

....

Read 2 Timothy 2:20–21, and write it out.

What is the large house Paul is referring to?

Does it surprise you that in the church there are honorable and dishonor-
able vessels?

In verse 21, what are the four ways Paul describes the instruments or the
vessels that the Master purposes to create?

What primary thing has to happen to the vessel to become honorable and
useful?

....

For clay to fire properly, it must be free from harmful impurities. In its
natural state, clay is rarely suitable for making pottery. Unlike today,
the ancient potter of Jeremiah's day could not purchase purified clay.
The raw earth had to be harvested from local clay deposits. When the
prophet Jeremiah visited the potter's house, he did not see the hard
work of quarrying clay. However, either earlier that day or the previous

one, the artist had taken his handcart to the rich terra-cotta deposits. In that local valley near Jerusalem, he had quarried his own clay and transported it back to his home. There he would mix the rough clay with water to form slurry, and then begin the process of purification. This cleansing involved removing extraneous matter such as soil, stones, or larger particles of debris.

In Romania, I watched Gregorio meticulously labor to purify the clay, even during the process of wheel throwing (the entire activity of shaping the clay on the wheel). With great patience, he removed the impurities that corrupted the integrity of the clay. Contamination produces disastrous results by leaving voids, gaps, and rough surfaces that degrade the integrity and aesthetics of the vessel. At times, contamination can completely destroy the clay.

Making pottery was a very common but incredibly important occupation in the ancient world. In the time of Jeremiah, clay-throwing artisans flourished as a profession. They utilized the so-called fast wheel, which first appeared around 1600 BC. According to Wendy Lawton's *Impressions in Clay*, this high-speed tool "consisted of two parallel stone or clay wheels connected by a shaft. As the potter moved the lower wheel with his bare feet, the upper wheel rotated smoothly."

Purposing to deal with His contaminated people, God likens Himself to a Potter throwing clay on the wheel.

••

Read Jeremiah 18:1–4. Describe in your own terms what it means for the clay to be marred.

What did the Potter do when He saw that the clay was marred?

How does it make you feel knowing the Potter is willing to start over and give the clay a second chance?

••

Jeremiah was accustomed to hearing from Yahweh in the ordinary events of daily life. He had already received a word from the Lord through an almond shoot and boiling pot (Jeremiah 1:11–14). In chapter 18, God spoke through a potter. Undoubtedly, Jeremiah had seen a potter at work many times. But this day was different. Through a living illustration, God revealed His grace in a special way. As the piece began to take shape, the potter realized the clay was marred. So, he pressed the flawed vessel back into a lump of clay and started over. Once again, God painted an incredibly clear picture for Jeremiah and His people. Because of sin, His heavy hand of discipline is imminent. However, the opportunity to change remains, because grace abounds.

spiritual inventory

Is the clay of your life pure or marred? _____

_____

_____

_____

_____

_____

Are there any known sins that you need to confess and forsake?

_____

_____

_____

_____

_____

_____

_____

If yes, how about closing out today by taking a moment to agree with God about your impurities? Ask Him for forgiveness and renewal. (See 1 John 1:9.)

Day 2
Grace Abounds

As a young man, Jeremiah experienced firsthand how God graciously reshapes marred clay. Born toward the end of King Manasseh's rule, Jeremiah grew up in a corrupt and spiritually dark context. His prophetic ministry began in 627 BC during the thirteenth year of King Josiah's reign (640–609 BC), and it spanned the rule of five kings, concluding in 587 BC (Jeremiah 1:2–3). The Bible tells us that "Josiah was eight years old when he became king, and he reigned in Jerusalem thirty-one years" (2 Kings 22:1). Josiah had his work cut out for him. His grandfather Manasseh (697–642 BC) and father Amon (642–640 BC) had led the kingdom of Judah into utter apostasy. Judah's apostasy included human sacrifice, idolatry, and superstitious cultic practices. In fact, Scripture describes Manasseh as deplorable: "Manasseh led them astray, so that they did more evil than the nations the LORD had destroyed before the Israelites" (2 Kings 21:9).

Read 2 Chronicles 34:1–8, and describe how Josiah progressively reformed worship in Israel.

What is significant about Josiah's efforts, and what does it teach us about where spiritual renewal begins?

In 622 BC, while craftsmen labored to renovate the place of worship, Hilkiah the high priest found the Book of the Law in the temple of the Lord. He immediately had it delivered to the king and the reform continued.

Read 2 Chronicles 34:19–21. What is the biblical significance of Josiah tearing his robes?

Why, when hearing the words of the Law, was Josiah's heart so broken?

Read 2 Chronicles 34:26–28. How did God honor the responsive heart of the king?

Take some time to fill in the blanks below and list the qualities that identified Josiah as a receptive and pliable vessel as recorded in 2 Chronicles 34:27.

Josiah's heart was _____ .

Josiah _____ before God.

Josiah _____ what God spoke.

What does God promise Josiah because of his spiritual receptivity?

Read 2 Chronicles 34:29–33, and outline the action steps Josiah took in response to his brokenness.

••••••••••••••••••••••••••••••••••••••

In response to the grace of God, Josiah launched one of the greatest spiritual awakenings in Israel's history. The revival involved eliminating any impurities in the contaminated clay of God's people. From 622–609 BC, the rebirth included the kingdom of Judah renewing its covenant with the Lord (2 Kings 23:1–3). For nearly two decades, Josiah served with the relentless passion of purifying a people for God. According to biblical scholar John Bright, "Never had there been a reform so sweeping in its aims and so consistent in its execution!"

••••••••••••••••••••••••••••••••••••••

Read the following two passages of Scripture that summarize Josiah's legacy.

2 Kings 22:2

2 Kings 23:25

How does Josiah personally inspire you to leave a legacy for God?

••••••••••••••••••••••••••••••••••••••

Day 3
Marred Clay

For well over a decade, the prophet Jeremiah participated in this great awakening led by Josiah. He experienced the spiritual vitality that exists when God's people honor their covenant love relationship with the Lord. However, the fires of revival died out in 609 BC when Josiah was killed in battle by the Egyptians at Megiddo. Nearly two decades of spiritual reformation failed to overcome the notorious misrule that Josiah's father Amon and grandfather Manasseh had imposed on the kingdom of Judah.

To more fully comprehend grace and better capture what God was saying to Jeremiah, we must first answer a question: how corrupt had the clay of Judah become? The Hebrew word translated as "marred" is *shâchath*, which means, "destroy, corrupt, and utterly waste." This same verb is used in Jeremiah 13:7 where we read, "So I [Jeremiah] went to Perath and dug up the belt and took it from the place where I had hidden it, but now it was ruined (*shâchath*) and completely useless." Further, Jack R. Lundbom states in his commentary on Jeremiah that "many commentators and translations . . . assume iterative tenses of these verbs, which means that Jeremiah is observing more than one failure during his visit."

In chapters 2–20, the prophet addresses Israel's ongoing depravity through numerous messages that come directly from the Lord. The first communication is a passionate appeal from God in Jeremiah 2:1–2.

> The word of the LORD came to me: "Go and proclaim in the hearing of Jerusalem . . . 'I remember the devotion of your youth, how as a bride you loved me and followed me through the wilderness, through a land not sown.'"

••••••••••••••••••••••••••••••••••••••

In Jeremiah 2:1–2, what metaphor does God use to describe His relationship with His people?

Why does God say, "I remember the devotion of your youth"?

••••••••••••••••••••••••••••••••••••••

In Jeremiah 3:1 God magnifies Judah's broken relationship with Him saying, "But you have lived as a prostitute with many lovers—would you now return to me?"

....

What was God referring to when he says Judah prostituted herself with "many lovers"?

Read Exodus 20:3–4, and describe why idolatry is so offensive to God.

God's jealousy portrays a loving and devoted husband concerned that his wife has cheated on him. Why is a godly jealousy necessary in a marital relationship?

In Revelation 2:4 how does Jesus, the bridegroom, express His jealousy to His bride in Ephesus?

In Revelation 2:5 Jesus presents three action steps for renewing a first love relationship with the bridegroom. List the three steps and comment on why they are necessary.

1. _____

2. _____

3. _____

....

Israel's apostasy is further depicted as God sends the prophet on a fact-finding mission:

> Go up and down the streets of Jerusalem, look around and consider, search through her squares. If you can find but one person who deals honestly and seeks the truth, I will forgive this city.
> —Jeremiah 5:1

....

Does it shock you to know that even after all the reforms Josiah set in place, Jeremiah could not find one person who lived with integrity?

....

The capstone of abandonment and immorality is recorded in Jeremiah's famous Temple sermon (Jeremiah 7:2–15), which is precisely dated 609–608 BC (Jeremiah 26:1). Strikingly, Jeremiah preached this message only a few months after Josiah's death. God's words to Judah are sobering:

"Will you steal and murder, commit adultery and perjury, burn incense to Baal and follow other gods you have not known, and then come and stand before me in this house, which bears my Name, and say, 'We are safe'—safe to do all these detestable things? Has this house, which bears my Name, become a den of robbers to you? But I have been watching!" declares the LORD. "Go now to the place in Shiloh where I first made a dwelling for my Name, and see what I did to it because of the wickedness of my people Israel." —Jeremiah 7:9–12

⋯⋯⋯⋯⋯⋯⋯⋯⋯⋯⋯⋯

List the sins Judah committed (recorded in Jeremiah 7:9–12) that demonstrate how completely contaminated the clay became.

Read Jeremiah 3:6–10, and describe why the reforms in Judah were short-lived.

What does it mean that Judah returned to the Lord only in "pretense"?

Give a few modern-day examples of how someone could superficially follow the Lord but in reality have their heart far from the Lord.

⋯⋯⋯⋯⋯⋯⋯⋯⋯⋯⋯⋯

So, standing at the entrance to the potter's house, Jeremiah was once again reminded that the potter does not quickly give up on the clay. He does not discard the clay—even though it is utterly impure. Neither does he abandon the clay out of frustration, and thankfully, he does not throw the corrupted clay away. As Jeremiah watched, the potter gently picked up the clay and "formed it into another pot, shaping it as seemed best to him" (Jeremiah 18:4). The lesson is obvious. Although the clay did not deserve another chance for usefulness, the Heavenly Potter demonstrated grace and a willingness to reshape the ruined piece. In the *Bible Reader's Companion*, Larry Richards insightfully states:

> The message God intended to communicate through this illustration from ancient life was not, as some have thought, one of divine sovereignty. It was a message of grace. Judah had resisted the divine potter. Yet even now God was willing to begin anew and reshape His people into that good vessel He had in mind from the beginning.

Take a moment to reflect on the graciousness of God, and write a prayer of thanksgiving expressing your appreciation to the Lord.

Day 4
Let God's Grace Amaze You

This image of God shaping and reshaping the clay of our lives opens for us a window to discern more clearly the loving heart of the Potter. The Master Potter had already introduced Himself to Jeremiah as *Yatsar* (Creator): "Before I formed [*yatsar*] you in the womb I knew you, before you were born I set you apart; I appointed you as a prophet to the nations" (Jeremiah 1:5). The potter launched Jeremiah's prophetic ministry using this graphic and intimate metaphor. It became a constant reminder that he was formed by God and had already spent time on the Potter's wheel, even before birth. His life was not an accident or a series of random circumstances. On the contrary, God had a divine plan for His people that first began on the Potter's wheel, with a person named Jeremiah.

A few decades passed, and his Maker continued purposeful communication, bridging the gap between the then and the now. "Go to the potter's house," He commanded. "Go, Jeremiah, and let your imagination run free. Watch the potter at work, and let me etch into your mind a picture of My love, grace, and mercy toward My people." In obedience, Jeremiah entered the potter's studio. As he intently watched the clay being remade, he was once again reminded of the potter's gracious disposition. Although the clay was marred, the potter looked at it with eyes of hope, not despair. I have heard it said that; "Grace is the face God wears when He looks at our failures." Can you see, as Jeremiah did, the face of a benevolent God who looks at His unfavorable people with eyes of favor? In a *Discipleship Journal* article titled "Pottery Training," Sue Kline captures the charitable heart of the Potter and the spirit of this passage:

> How many of us, I wonder, have quit growing spiritually simply because we are worn out? And in our fatigue, how many of us have assumed that God is worn out, too? . . . One of these days, I half believe, He's going to step back from His potter's wheel, shake His head sadly, and write me off as an intractable lump of clay. . . . I encourage you to stay on that wheel . . . He only creates masterpieces.

So, once more, the Father's benevolence shines through: He offers grace by demonstrating His willingness to mold us again, into vessels of honor fit for His use. The famous Scottish preacher Alexander Whyte used to say that the victorious Christian life was "a series of new beginnings." Because of grace, that is what the Potter is offering His people. This fresh start always begins with the Potter. He is the initiator. However, it also requires the contaminated clay to respond favorably. Through repentance, surrender, and yielding to the kind efforts of the Potter, the clay can be made new.

••

Read Luke 22:54–62, and describe why Peter is a perfect example of God's amazing grace.

Read John 21:15–19. How did Jesus administer grace to Peter?

From your understanding of grace, why is it so amazing?

Do you need a fresh start like Peter did?

••

Grace to Repent

According to Phillip J. King, no prophet had more to say about repentance than Jeremiah. The Hebrew word for repentance is *šub*, most often translated as "return" or "turn." The word *šub* appears 111 times in Jeremiah and is the twelfth most frequently used verb in the Old Testament, thus elevating its doctrinal importance in Scripture. Repentance implies turning from sin to righteousness. It involves a sorrowful reorientation of a person's life toward God. Genuine contrition leads to a lifestyle of no regrets because it ultimately restores one's love relationship with the Lord (Revelation 2:4–5) and renews the joy of their salvation (Psalm 51:7–12).

God's passionate plea for His people to return is packaged in the most endearing terms. "'Return, faithless people,' declares the LORD, 'for I am your husband'" (Jeremiah 3:14). God's appeal to Judah could not be clearer or kinder. As a zealous husband, He comes urging a wayward wife to restore the shattered love relationship. Now, the Master Potter reframes His appeal for repentance, bringing further clarity through the analogy of potter and clay. The Potter makes it clear that His plea will have one of two conclusions: pardon for repentance or discipline for continued disobedience.

> Like clay in the hand of the potter, so are you in my hand, Israel. If at any time I announce that a nation or kingdom is to be uprooted, torn down and destroyed, and if that nation I warned repents of its evil, then I will relent and not inflict on it the disaster I had planned. And if at another time I announce that a nation or kingdom is to be built up and planted, and if it does evil in my sight and does not obey me, then I will reconsider the good I had intended to do for it. —Jeremiah 18:6–10

Notice how willing God is to exercise grace. He tells Jeremiah "if at any time" sinners genuinely repent, He will curtail His righteous judgments. The NIV rightly translates the word "relent" from the Hebrew word *nakham*. The root meaning of *nakham* promotes the idea of "breathing deeply" and depicts the "physical display of one's feelings, usually sorrow, compassion, or comfort." The revelation from the potter's house suggests that God's grief is so deep toward sinful humanity that He promises to modify His sovereign decrees when sinners repent. This passage demonstrates that Israel's response really matters: the Potter promises to change His decree because of genuine repentance. Yahweh's mind does not change; however, His treatment of repentant sinners does.

Repentance has always been the first word, and initial step, back to God. Both John the Baptist and Jesus preached, "Repent, for the kingdom of heaven has come near" (Matthew 3:2; 4:17). The first sermon proclaimed by Peter in the Book of Acts calls people to "repent and be baptized" (Acts 2:38). Jeremiah learned, as all people must, that when people submit to God's purposes it results in the Potter making something beautiful out of them. According to Jack Hayford in the *Spirit-filled Life Student Bible*, yielded clay in the hands of the Potter produces an eternal quality that "rebellious 'clay' will never find." These immortal virtues include brokenness, humility, and surrender to the faithful efforts of the Potter.

Repentance is a choice. The clay must decide who and what will control its destiny. Would Judah respond to God's jealous appeal? Would God's kindness lead its people to repentance (Romans 2:4)? As the Potter continues reshaping the marred clay, he relays the following message through the prophet:

> Now therefore say to the people of Judah and those living in Jerusalem, "This is what the LORD says: Look! I am preparing a disaster for you and devising a plan against you. So turn from your evil ways, each one of you, and reform your ways and your actions." But they will reply, "It's no use. We will continue with our own plans; we will all follow the stubbornness of our evil hearts."
> —Jeremiah 18:11–12

....

Have you ever experienced a time when you resisted the work of God's Spirit and lived with a stubborn and sinful heart?

What was that experience like? How did God overcome the hardness of your heart?

....

Day 5
Grace and Truth

I vividly remember the first time I sat at a potter's wheel. Getting comfortable was not easy. I had to stoop low. It felt awkward, trying to settle in around the clay. That position of stooping continued through the whole process of throwing clay. At the heart of grace, as Chuck Swindoll describes in *Grace Awakening*, is God's ability to "bend" or to "stoop." Likewise, Donald Barnhouse taught, "Love that goes upward is worship, love that goes outward is affection; love that stoops is grace." Jeremiah watched the potter stooping and visually experienced the Artisan's grace in remaking the marred vessel. But, Jeremiah's time in the potter's house also included a bold proclamation of truth: if Judah does not repent, discipline is imminent.

I have discovered that most people embrace the God of grace but neglect and even resent, at times, the God of truth. Grace is comfortable and welcoming because it offers what we do not deserve. The root word for *grace* in Greek signifies "unmerited favor, undeserved blessing, a free gift." Everyone enjoys receiving gifts. However, we must understand that we cannot take God in slices. He is a God of both grace and truth. C. S. Lewis captures these complementary virtues of grace and truth in his classic work *The Lion, the Witch and the Wardrobe*. In a conversation with Mr. and Mrs. Beaver, Lucy inquires about the lion, Aslan, his attributes, and what it would be like to meet him.

"Is he—quite safe? I shall feel rather nervous about meeting a lion."

"That you will dearie, and no mistake," said Mrs. Beaver; "if there's anyone who can appear before Aslan without their knees knocking, they're either braver than most or just silly."

"Then he isn't safe?" said Lucy.

"Safe?" said Mr. Beaver; "don't you hear what Mrs. Beaver tells you? Who said anything about safe? 'Course he isn't safe. But he's good. He's the King, I tell you."

Yes, God is good, kind, merciful, long-suffering, compassionate, and full of grace. However, we must understand, as C. S. Lewis did, that He is not "safe." His absolute holiness places legal requirements on our lives that are presented throughout Scripture. Grace without truth leads to emotionalism, apathy, and moral indifference. That is why Dallas Willard prophetically declares in his article "Spiritual Formation: What it is, and How it is Done," "We're not only saved by grace, we're paralyzed by it." The Bible, along with church history, is replete with examples of grace abuse. Some disciples in the early church began confusing God's grace with a license to live lawlessly. Paul countered this heresy inquiring, "What shall we say, then? Shall we go on sinning so that grace may increase? By no means! We are those who have died to sin; how can we live in it any longer?" (Romans 6:1–2).

On the flip side, truth without grace promotes a heavy-hammered and legalistic spirit, which dulls the power of the gospel. Martin Luther wrote, "The devil doesn't care which side of the horse we fall off of—as long as we don't stay in the saddle. We need to mount the horse with one foot in the stirrup of truth, the other in the stirrup of grace."

....

Jesus lived the perfect equilibrium of grace and truth. *Write out John 1:14.*

Read John 8:1–12, and describe how Jesus rightly balanced grace while ministering to the woman caught in adultery.

....

No other people group had experienced the favor of God as the nation of Israel did. Because of grace, Yahweh chose them as His covenant people (Genesis 12:1–3) and entrusted them "with the very words of God" (Romans 3:2). Yet, Judah chose to trample on God's grace saying: "It's no use. We will continue with our own plans; we will all follow the stubbornness of our evil hearts" (Jeremiah 18:12; and see 2:25). Scripture summarizes their grace abuse with a sobering statement reiterated nine different times, stating that Judah "did not listen" to the Lord (Jeremiah 7:13, 24, 26; 11:8; 17:23; 25:7; 34:14; 35:17; 44:5). As God originally promised, the totality of Jeremiah's preaching fell on deaf ears and spiritually unresponsive hearts. All hope for the immediate renewal of Israel ended not because Yahweh was unwilling and hardened but rather because His people were unwilling and hardened.

Through poetry, God presented His truth behind the coming judgment. Because Judah had "forgotten" the Lord (Jeremiah 3:21; 13:25; 18:15), God would show Judah His "back" and not His "face" in "the day of their disaster" (18:17). Since Israel refused to be reshaped, the Potter would plop the clay down and walk away, relegating the clay to its natural, hardened state. In Jeremiah 19, the Potter finalized His discipline of the marred clay. He instructed the prophet to purchase a clay pot to illustrate His divine activity graphically, once again. Jeremiah took the jar, along with the elders and priests, to the Valley of Ben Hinnom, just outside the Potsherd Gate in Jerusalem. Upon arrival, the prophet announced disaster on Judah and Jerusalem. Then he smashed the clay vessel to the ground. This smashing made it clear to all that God would destroy Judah by taking them into captivity, which He did in 587 BC through Nebuchadnezzar of Babylon (2 Chronicles 36:16–21). The Israelites followed their stubborn intentions all the way into exile as they left behind the ruins of God's Temple and the destruction of the Holy City of Jerusalem.

In August of 2004, I flew with my family to Fort Lauderdale, Florida, to officiate the wedding of some dear friends. We tacked on a week of vacation to enjoy the sights and sounds of the Florida Keys. However, Hurricane Frances abruptly changed our plans. As the storm approached, the governor of Florida mandated an evacuation. Although we struggled to interrupt our family vacation, we complied with the sobering directive of the authorities. Our flights were cancelled, so we rented a vehicle and headed north fast. The state of Florida had its act together, providing a clear and orderly evacuation plan. Even the tollbooths supported the process, as all traffic going north traveled through without delay or cost. As people embraced the strategic exodus, many lives were saved. However, there were some individuals who resisted the warnings, resulting in tragedy. As a category-four hurricane, Frances claimed approximately 47 lives and cost a total of $9 billion. Our family and thousands of others rushed to safety by heeding the mandated departure. Through grace, God warned Judah and offered an evacuation plan. But, the hardened clay of Israel would not listen. The people defiantly threw up their hands and said, "It's no use." They preferred to experience the consequences of their sin instead of experiencing the grace of God through repentance and faith.

••

Why do you think the people of Judah threw their hands up and chose not to respond to God's evacuation plan?

Does God give up, and should we give up on people whose hearts are hardened toward Him?

••

Day 6
Grace—The Last Word

Because of grace, the Book of Jeremiah does not end on a note of hopelessness. God did not abandon His people forever. Although His hand seemed heavy, it was still a hand of grace. Even in captivity, grace abounds. In the words of the Apostle John, "For from his fullness we have all received, grace upon grace" (John 1:16 ESV). Two of the most endearing passages from the Book of Jeremiah remind us that grace is the last word for the people of God.

....

Read Jeremiah 29:10–13 and *Jeremiah 31:31–34,* and answer the following questions.

How do you think Israel felt knowing the Lord had not abandoned them forever?

What must we learn about God from these beautiful passages of grace and hope?

Why do you think God continues to "stoop" low and offer a future for His people?

....

Grace—It Truly Is Amazing

The classic musical *Les Misérables*, based on the novel by Victor Hugo, came to the big screen December 25, 2012. How fitting for a movie filled with Christian virtue to debut the day we celebrate Christ's birth. *Les Misérables* is the story of a peasant thief named Jean Valjean who is incarcerated for stealing a loaf of bread. The movie opens with Valjean exiting prison. He wanders into a nearby village, and upon finding a home belonging to a clergyman, he requests lodging for the evening. Although the bishop knows nothing of this man, he shows benevolence by welcoming him into his home.

Late that evening Valjean continues his life of crime by filling his satchel with valuable silverware before leaving. His scoundrel activity startles the clergyman, who rises only to be accosted by the criminal.

Valjean knocks him out and flees with the goods. In the next scene, Valjean is arrested by the local police, who find the silverware in his sack. Their suspicion heightens as they identify the engraved initials on the treasures as that of the local cleric. The officers takes Valjean to the bishop's house and inquire, "We found this silverware and he says it belongs to him. But it must be yours, Reverend, isn't it? It has your initials on it." The minister walks over to the officer and, much to everyone's surprise, says, "No, he's right. This is his. It is my gift to him." Then, as if that gift was not enough, the preacher presents candlesticks that he declares Valjean "accidentally left behind." The bishop stooped low to honor Valjean. Instead of administering justice, he offered grace. However, this magnificent scene closes with the necessary and truthful response to grace as the bishop declares, "Jean Valjean, with this silver I have purchased your soul. Now go and make something redeeming out of it." Hugo understood the power of grace and truth. When properly embraced, God's grace and truth transform the most hardened heart. The bishop's offer of grace came packaged with the truth that redemption meant abandoning a life of sin.

Grace—My Story

....

Write out Isaiah 30:18.

What does this verse tell us about the heart of God?

....

How fabulous it is to know God yearns for us to respond to His grace. Although I grew up a cultural Christian for the first 19 years of my life, I knew little of the grace of God. I lived, as many Americans do, with a self-serving agenda. Independent of the Potter's gracious hands, I pursued a "TGIF mantra." However, the partying scene began to manifest its bankruptcy as loneliness, emptiness, and a lack of purpose filled my broken vessel. During those desolate days, the Lord initiated His amazing grace. His kind hands began to wedge the hardened clay of my life. Over time, as the Potter persisted, I began yielding to His tender efforts. After about a year of His faithful devotion, I finally said to the Potter, "Please, center the clay of my life and remake me a vessel for Your glory." Wow, the Master Potter got busy. The clay of my life began to take shape with meaning, hope, and purpose. The streetwise, drug-dealing, lascivious young adult experienced the Potter's winsome hands. More than three and a half decades have passed, but the Potter continues to wedge, mold, shape, crush, purify, glaze, and fire the clay of my life.

Grace—Our Response

Like Jeremiah and the nation of Israel, you are invited to come to the Potter's house and experience the grace of God. He will take your marred clay and remake it through the precious blood of His Son Jesus Christ. However, your response must be different from Israel's. God called Judah to turn from its sinful ways, and that invitation continues today. Jesus launched His public ministry by declaring as Jeremiah did, "Repent, for the kingdom of heaven has come near" (Matthew 4:17).

Do you see your need to be remade by the Heavenly Potter?

Do you recognize your sin has offended and separated you from a holy and righteous God (Isaiah 59:2)?

Are you willing to turn from your sin and put your faith and trust in the Savior (Acts 20:19–21)?

The Apostle John wrote, "Yet to all who did receive him, to those who believed in his name, he gave the right to become children of God" (John 1:12). The Potter's hands are opened wide. Will you yield to His gracious longing to shape your life through His Son Jesus Christ (Psalm 95:6–9)?

When I became a Christian, I cried out to the Lord in prayer. That prayer reflected the work of repentance that God had already accomplished in my heart. If you are ready to turn from your sins and trust in Christ alone, I encourage you to call upon the name of the Lord and experience His amazing grace.

Father,
I thank You for Your amazing grace. I recognize
that the clay of my life is marred, but I also recognize
that in Christ I can be made new. Therefore, I repent of
my sins and by faith trust Jesus Christ as my Savior
and Lord. Thank You for the gift of forgiveness, including
past, present, and future sins. Make me into the vessel
You want me to be. In Jesus' name.
Amen.

WEEK 6

DURABILITY: *Never, Ever Give Up*

PHILIPPIANS 2:12–18

Christianity without discipleship is always
Christianity without Christ.
—Dietrich Bonhoeffer

Day 1
Stick-to-it-iveness

On September 2, 2013, looking dazed and sunburned, 64-year-old United States endurance swimmer Diana Nyad walked out of the water, onto the beach, and into the history books. Nyad became the first person to swim from Cuba to Florida without the help of a shark cage. Her dream of swimming the Florida Straits, a 110-mile trek, began in 1978 when she was 28 years old. After four attempts that fell short, Nyad persevered and achieved the impossible. Hundreds of fans greeted her and celebrated the history-making event. Before being rushed to the local hospital by ambulance, she wanted the world to hear these words: "Never, ever give up."

Luke records that Mark, a teammate of Paul and Barnabas, aborted mission. Acts 15:36 records,

> **Some time later Paul said to Barnabas, "Let us go back and visit the believers in all the towns where we preached the word of the Lord and see how they are doing."**

Barnabas wanted to take John, also called Mark, with them, but Paul did not think it wise to take him, because he had deserted them in Pamphylia and not continued with them in the work. They had such a sharp disagreement that they parted company. Barnabas took Mark and sailed for Cyprus, but Paul chose Silas and left, commended by the brothers to the grace of the Lord. He went through Syria and Cilicia, strengthening the churches.

••••••••••••••••••••••••••••••••••••••

From what you know about Paul's missionary journeys, why do you think Mark deserted the mission?

Have you ever felt like throwing in the towel on a specific aspect of your faith journey?

What prompted the desire to quit, and how did things work out?

••••••••••••••••••••••••••••••••••••••

Clay becomes an enduring substance only after it is exposed to a high temperature. A clay vessel that has simply been sun-dried will eventually collapse if exposed to water. However, when clay is heated to a temperature usually around 1,290°F (700°C), its chemical composition and physical characteristics change permanently. Only after firing can the clay vessel be called pottery.

If you traveled to Turkey and toured the ruins of the ancient city of Troy (famous for the Trojan horse), you would find that the city was built and destroyed seven times. It would be built, but then an earthquake would reduce it to rubble. It would be rebuilt, and then the harbor would recede too far from the city to make it accessible to seafaring ships. However, one of its destructions created a positive lesson. As ancient walls reveal, at one time Troy burned to the ground, but in the process the enormous heat glazed many of the clay bricks used to build the homes and walls. Accidentally, the Trojans discovered that intensive heat works to cure and harden clay objects while also giving them a decorative sheen.

About 5,000 years ago, Chinese and Japanese potters began firing stoneware to higher temperatures, enabling the artisans to create vessels that would last lifetimes. Archeology has demonstrated that fired clay is not affected like wood and metal. Though a clay artifact may have been buried in the earth for thousands of years, it remains in exactly the same shape and condition as when first fired. As the temperature rises, the clay becomes denser, harder, and more durable. The divine value behind God firing the clay of our lives is His desire to see us live durably and persevere as vessels of honor fit for His use. The Apostle Paul championed the attributes of endurance and durability as lasting marks of the Potter's hands on the clay.

••••••••••••••••••••••••••••••••••••••

Read Romans 5:3–4. According to the Apostle Paul, what role does suffering play in developing perseverance?

What is the ultimate goal of perseverance?

••••••••••••••••••••••••••••••••••••••

The Greek term for character is *dokime*, and it literally describes someone or something that has been put to the test and proven "genuine." Ancient potters stamped *dokimas* on the bottom of pottery, indicating the piece had endured firing and met the highest standards of quality, thus making it durable and ready for use. Every authentic Christ follower must experience the heat of discipleship to insure durability and perseverance of faith.

Now, perseverance of the saints does not suggest that Christians are completely free from the entanglements and setbacks sin affords. A simple analysis of Scripture quickly reminds us that not all believers equally endure the race set before them and demonstrate that there are various levels of "stick-to-it-iveness."

In seminary, I had the privilege to study under Dr. Robert Clinton. He has devoted the better part of his ministry to examining the durability of leaders in Scripture. His study clearly reveals the tension that exists between levels of steadfastness. Clinton developed case studies on hundreds of leaders. His curiosity focused on one thing: how many of God's front-runners finished well. He narrowed his research to 49 individuals from Scripture who revealed enough information to determine their level of spiritual fortitude.

He outlined four different kinds of finishes: those who were cut off early, those who finished poorly, those who finished so-so, and, finally, those who finished well. His research is exceptional and motivational for leaders but his conclusion are alarming.

In the following chart, see if you can match the individual with how they finished their faith journey. If you need support read the adjacent Scriptures.

Individual	Cut off early	Finished poorly	Finished so-so	Finished well
Joshua (Joshua 24:29–31)				
Eli (1 Samuel 4:12–22)				
David (2 Samuel 12:1–25)				
Absalom (2 Samuel 18:9–17)				

Individual	Cut off early	Finished poorly	Finished so-so	Finished well
Solomon (1 Kings 11:1–13)				
Ananias & Sapphira (Acts 5:1–11)				
Paul (2 Timothy 4:6–8)				
Demas (2 Timothy 4:9–10)				

spiritual inventory

It is sobering to examine biblical history and realize that many of those who started well finished less favorably. Given your current spiritual trajectory, are you poised to finish well? _____

_____

_____

_____

_____

Are there any adjustments you need to make? _____

_____

_____

_____

_____

Day 2
Finishing Well

When the Apostle Paul wrote to the church members at Philippi, he was encouraged by their spiritual progress. He commended them for their partnership in the gospel (Philippians 1:5) and their continuity of faith (2:12). Ten years had passed since he'd planted the church in Philippi. These believers were on their way to finishing well. Paul never took their spiritual progress for granted but instead exhorted them to continue on in the faith.

....

Read Philippians 2:12–13, and answer the following questions.

From verse 12, describe the role a believer plays in their own spiritual development.

From verse 13, describe the complementary role God plays in our faith formation.

What does the phrase "work out" imply in this passage?

....

Paul was writing to Christians, exhorting them to work "out," not work "for," their redemption. Paul longed for the church to live with durability and continuity of faith.

I learned a great lesson on going the distance while writing my doctoral dissertation. After many months of research, writing, praying, and editing, the time finally came to submit the first three chapters of the dissertation to my mentor. Extremely excited but wondering how my advisor would respond to my work, I remained on the edge of my seat for the next few weeks. To my dismay, the paper returned very bloodied. The capstone of discouragement came when a note from my mentor demanded, "Keith, your first three chapters are too long. Edit your work to 95 pages." Frustration filled every ounce of red and white blood cells flowing through my body.

"Eliminate 45 pages—are you kidding?" I told my wife. "That's it. I quit. I'm done. Dissertation writing is not my thing."

Thankfully, after a few days break, some solid encouragement from my wife, and time in prayer with the Lord, I got back into the game and finished well.

....

Read 1 Thessalonians 3:6–8, and describe the importance Paul places on continuity and perseverance of faith.

According to Acts 17:1–10, Paul and Silas had a brief ministry experience in Thessalonica. With that in mind, why do you think Timothy's progress report was so important to Paul?

Describe the report Timothy gave to Paul about the church at Thessalonica.

What news did Paul receive that brought him life and great encouragement in ministry?

What does it mean to stand firm in the Lord?

If a close friend were presenting your spiritual progress report, would it be affirming?

....

Day 3
Follow Christ

Finishing well necessitates following the steadfast obedient model of Christ.

••••••••••••••••••••••••••••••••

Write out Hebrews 12:1-2, and answer the following questions.

What does it mean to "fix" our eyes on Jesus?

How does fixing our eyes on Jesus help us persevere and finish the race well?

What does it mean that Jesus "endured" the Cross?

Do you think Jesus struggled as He purposed to finish well?

••••••••••••••••••••••••••••••••

When we focus on Jesus, the standard for discipleship stays fixed. We measure our spirituality against Him and put aside comparison to others. When our attention is on Christ, we quickly discover that finishing strong is "a long obedience in the same direction," a phrase used by Friedrich Nietzsche to describe the essential purposes of individuals and described more fully in a Eugene Peterson book by the same name. Consider for a moment the tumultuous but faithful bookends of Christ's public ministry. It began with 40 days in the Judean wilderness that included intense spiritual assaults (Matthew 4:1–11) and climaxed in Gethsemane, where He agonized over the implications of Calvary by sweating drops of blood (Luke 22:44). Has anyone ever experienced such spiritual anguish? That agony culminated at Golgotha when Jesus cried from the Cross, "My God, my God, why have you forsaken me?" (Matthew 27:46). Jesus models for us that there are no shortcuts or quick fixes for discipleship. In a culture that values immediate gratification, we must view our faith journey more like a marathon than a sprint. The Apostle Paul clarified that sanctification is the process of being transformed from glory to glory (2 Corinthians 3:18). That is why our starting point necessitates a relationship with Christ, who lived in continuous obedience to His Father. Persevering to the end is a reflection of our spiritual journey today, how obedient a life we are living right now.

The faith journey of King David demonstrates that our walk today impacts our tomorrow and our ability to finish well. I would contend that Scripture portrays King David as finishing so-so. David set the course of his mediocre finish the moment he married a second wife. Then he married a third. By that time he was on a roll and married a fourth, followed by a fifth, then a sixth. According to Scripture, his family mushroomed to include eight wives, ten concubines, 21 sons, and one daughter, and that number does not include children from the concubines. For many years David violated the revealed will of God outlined in the Pentateuch, which states,

> When you enter the land the Lord your God is giving you and have taken possession of it and settled in it, and you say, "Let us set a king over us like all the nations around us," be sure to appoint over you a king the Lord your God chooses . . . He must not take many wives, or his heart will be led astray.
> —Deuteronomy 17:14–17

Due to his polygamist lifestyle, David's clay vessel had a fair amount of cracks. His downhill spiral seemed at its worst when he committed adultery with Bathsheba. Then he tried covering his tracks by murdering her husband, Uriah, one of his colleagues and "mighty men."

David's haphazard routine should challenge us to examine ourselves, to see if there are any patterns or sinful habits in our lives today that will keep us from finishing strong. We must take time to inventory our spiritual journey and progress of faith by reflecting on God's righteous commands to see if we are willfully violating any of them. David reminds us that every decision today will impact tomorrow and our ability to go the distance. In *Staying Faithful through the Years*, Jerry Bridges strengthens the argument for honest assessment in order to finish strong:

> We do not suddenly become something in our sixties that we have not been moving toward throughout our lifetimes. *All of us are going to be tomorrow what we are becoming today.* To stay faithful through the years means that we are staying on track today and will continue to do so tomorrow . . . and next week . . . and in the months and years ahead. We must set our sights now on endurance.

Billy Graham turned 97 on November 7, 2015. Dr. Graham exemplifies the truth that our tomorrow is intimately connected to today. David Aikman, in *Great Souls*, looks in the rearview mirror, to 1948, and Modesto, California. In Modesto, the spirited evangelist assembled his inner three—George Beverly Shea, Grady Wilson, and Cliff Barrows—for a watershed meeting. Graham initiated the summit, proposing to deal with the challenges, successes, and temptations of a burgeoning crusade ministry. That summit established an uncompromising system that safeguarded their marriages, testimony, and gospel ministry for more than six decades.

Aikman summarizes what came to be called the Modesto Manifesto. Regarding finances, the team established that the local leadership would take care of the money and pay the evangelists. In regard to temptation while traveling away from their wives, each affirmed he would never be alone with any woman who was not his wife, regardless of the setting. In regard to results, they all agreed never to give in to gross exaggeration of crusade numbers. Whenever possible, the local police or other officials reported the statistics. The Modesto Manifesto set standards for public evangelism. It proactively countered the fiery darts of the devil, as it pertained to the "'three g's' that have wrecked so many promising careers in Christian ministry: gold, girls, and glory."

The enduring evangelist embraced the truth that finishing well starts today. He raised the bar for Christian ministry by exemplifying integrity and trust, which are foundational for any enduring service to the Lord. A long obedience in the same direction requires a "stick-to-it-iveness" grounded in biblical truth that gets fleshed out as our risen Savior sanctifies us on a daily basis. Keeping the faith demands we abandon the sprint mentality and run the spiritual marathon set before us.

••••••••••••••••••••••••••••••••••••

Read John 17:4, and describe how Jesus defined going the distance.

Do you, like Jesus, desire to glorify God by finishing the work He gave you to do?

Based on your current lifestyle, will you complete the work He gave you to do and finish well?

••••••••••••••••••••••••••••••••••••

Day 4
All In

Seo Sang-moon gives new meaning to the idea of "stick-to-it-ive-ness" and going all in. He never flinched at his determination to pass his driver's license examination. Seo immigrated to the United States from rural South Korea. He struggled to pass a written examination because of illiteracy, but his tenacious spirit motivated him to take his oral examination as often as possible in order to learn the rules of the road. At 69, he reached his goal after 272 attempts and nearly $1,000 in administrative fees. Seo Sang-moon never, ever gave up.

According to Philippians 2:12–13, the clay has a responsibility to participate and work with the Potter as He shapes worthy vessels. The phrase "working out our salvation" carries with it the idea of a working out to completion, to ultimate fulfillment. This working out will involve a continuous sustained effort that every Christian must pursue.

The Bible likens our spiritual journey to a partnership with God. I appreciate the story of the little boy who went to see a boxing match with his father. Within a few moments of the bout beginning, one of the fighters knelt down in his corner, made the sign of the cross, and prayed. The child asked his father, "Dad, does that help?" His dad replied, "Yes, if he can throw a punch."

The disciples of Christ do not live passive lifestyles. Yes, God calls us to pray, but He also demands we engage, do our part and act on our faith. The Christian boxing match takes effort. A boxer would never step into the ring trusting in petition alone. Prayer, preparation, and participation are all vitally important.

Yielded Clay

Paul states that God values the attitude of "fear and trembling" (Philippians 2:12) as we work out our salvation. Numerous Pauline epistles highlight these seasoned qualities, and the phrase *fear and trembling* can best be summarized by the word *humility*. (See 1 Corinthians 2:3; 2 Corinthians 7:15; Ephesians 6:5.) In 2 Corinthians 7:15; Ephesians 6:5; and Philippians 2:12; the expression is closely associated with "obedience." Notice, too, that Paul has just pointed out that Christ's *humility* was demonstrated by His *obedience* (Philippians 2:8). Now, why is humility essential to going the distance?

As we work out our own salvation, God is interested in both our actions and the attitudes behind our actions. Our deeds are what we outwardly do, but our disposition reflects who we inwardly are. The life of King Uzziah best illustrates how vital humility is to finishing well. Uzziah's reign over Judah began in 792 BC, when he was 16 years old, and lasted 52 years.

....

Read 2 Chronicles 26:1–5. Describe the faith journey of King Uzziah.

....

Initially, and in many ways, Uzziah led well, which resulted in God prospering him. He conquered the Philistines and fortified Jerusalem, along with the surrounding countryside. In addition, he built a mighty army and received tribute from vassal states. Clearly, Scripture suggests, Uzziah had a great start. But, there was a discontinuity in Uzziah's walk with God and it led to dire consequences.

....

Write out 2 Chronicles 26:15–16.

....

Uzziah reminds us that pride frequently accompanies achievement, whether in business, sports, scholastics, or kingdom endeavors. His arrogance brought ruin to his life and ministry. Proverbs 16:18 makes it clear: "Pride goes before destruction, a haughty spirit before a fall." Humility, however, will keep the clay of our lives soft and yielding in the Potter's hand.

In addition to humility, God requires clay to stay dependent in His hands because "it is God who works in [us] to will and to act according to his good purpose" (Philippians 2:13). The word *works* in this verse is translated from the Greek word *energeō*, a present active participle from which we ultimately get our English concept of "energizing." Our partnership with God involves our "working" while God does the "energizing." The almighty Potter provides the divine enablement that we must continually access, depend upon, and lean into. Paul uses the same Greek term to describe God's work in our lives while writing to the church at Colossae.

···

Write out Colossians 1:28–29.

···

Throughout the years various movements have promoted unique models of Christian discipleship and what it means to work out one's salvation. Three primary paradigms are best illustrated through a maritime metaphor. Think about the differences between a raft, a motorboat, and a sailboat. In a raft, you simply drift. You let the tide, water, and weather do whatever they will. No effort, no rowing, just drifting along in the sea of life and trusting the natural elements for guidance. You "let go and let God." In a motorboat, however, you are in control. You start the engine. You monitor the speed. You direct the path. You become the master of your destiny and the captain of your ship. Sailing is a much different picture and the best analogy of our dependent partnership with Christ. We are not passive when sailing, every sailor has a role to play. Roles that include steering the rudder, directing the mainsails, and tacking the boat. However, unlike someone in the motorboat or raft, a sailor is utterly dependent on the wind. There is no room for a sailor to believe he or she is in ultimate control because if the wind does not blow, the maritime vessel sits idle in the water. On the other hand, when the wind blows, filling the mainsail and jibe, amazing things can happen. May I suggest that the Christian partnership with God is much like sailing? We are dependent upon the wind of the Holy Spirit, but we have a significant partnership in this nautical journey. Jesus highlighted this divine cooperation, stating, "I am the vine; you are the branches. If you remain in me and I in you, you will bear much fruit; apart from me you can do nothing" (John 15:5).

I am aware that some of you reading this right now feel like giving up. You never anticipated the kiln getting so hot or the race being so arduous. Maybe you feel like many runners do midway through the Boston Marathon. Starting at mile 16, marathoners encounter a number of inclines, climaxing at mile marker 20.5 with the dreaded Heartbreak

Hill, the longest and steepest ascent in the race. What makes this climb excruciating is that world-class runners often "hit the wall" during the ascent. Runners testify that their muscles begin screaming for oxygen, and they literally feel like dying. Heartbreak Hill tests every ounce of a marathoner's determination and strength.

Because our faith journey is not run on a level grade, at times we hit the wall and want to bail. The loss of a job or of a home through foreclosure screams at us to quit. A daughter becomes pregnant out of wedlock or chooses cohabitation instead of marriage, and we feel like a failure. A loved one gets diagnosed with a terminal illness or unexpectedly dies, and loneliness and depression set in. The pain of divorce or a broken relationship results in feelings of desperation and the inability to finish well.

When you feel the heat of the kiln transforming the clay of your life and it seems unbearable, please remember God is working in you to bring about His good and perfect will. Stick with it. Never, ever give up. He will provide all the spiritual energy and resources you need to finish well. Do your part by yielding, by remaining humbly dependent on His divine enablement, so you can persevere to the end.

Day 5
Live Content

Write out Philippians 2:14.

In Philippians 2:14, Paul furthers his encouragement to finish well with an appeal to live contentedly. The phrase "do everything" refers to working out our salvation with fear and trembling. Now, you may be wondering what contentment has to do with finishing well. Have you ever considered that the source of grumbling and complaining is lack of satisfaction in a person's life? Isaiah warned Israel by saying,

> **Woe to those who quarrel with their Maker, those who are nothing but potsherds among the potsherds on the ground. Does the clay say to the potter, "What are you making?" Does your work say, "The potter has no hands"? —Isaiah 45:9**

Scripture teaches that contented people live durably and finish well. In contrast, people who grumble and complain frustrate perseverance because their lives are tainted with ongoing displeasure. God's Word is saturated with examples of how discontentment disrupts finishing well. The word translated "grumbling" in Philippians 2 is also used to describe Israel's whining in the wilderness (Exodus 16:7–9, 12; Numbers 17:5, 10).

Read Exodus 15:22–24, and answer the following questions.

What caused Israel to grumble against Moses?

Was their complaint legitimate?

Clearly, the nation of Israel demonstrates that often our discontentment stems from challenging circumstances in life. In our frustration with our spiritual journey, we regularly blame our difficulties on those around us. The people of God pointed their fingers at leadership and began the blame game. Moses wrote about their displaced aggression, stating, "In the desert the whole community grumbled against Moses and Aaron" (Exodus 16:2). Because hurting people hurt people, attacking leadership is a constant problem in all areas of life.

I have seen disgruntled parents lash out at teachers, coaches, and youth pastors because of their displeasure with how these figures handled certain issues with their kids. Further, I have counseled many dissatisfied spouses because their mates have fallen short of meeting their expectations. "If only they would meet my needs and make my life more palatable," they cry. John MacArthur writes, "mounting discontent through the years produces the trauma of a so-called 'mid-life crisis.'" Out of discontent, husbands pursue other women or try filling their void with recreational toys and activities. Midlife crisis is nothing more than midlife discontent with an individual's current state of affairs. Now, I wish the church had an exemption clause from such disgruntled behavior. Moses and Aaron provide a glimpse into the epidemic of unsatisfied saints in the church today. At one point the people's rage against Moses and Aaron culminated in "the whole assembly talk[ing] about stoning them" (Numbers 14:10). The sad reality about our unhappiness is that it ultimately reflects our irritation with God.

Write out Numbers 17:10–11.

God makes it clear that Israel's grumbling was ultimately directed toward the Lord Himself. Their caustic spirit spread like wildfire, as a few malcontents led to the disheartening of a whole community: "So the men Moses had sent to explore the land, who returned and made the whole community grumble against him by spreading a bad report about it" (Numbers 14:36).

These whiners paid the price for their rebellion because none of that current generation of Israelites, except Joshua and Caleb, entered the Promised Land (Numbers 14:20–25). Remember, finishing well is God's goal for every believer. However, only two faithful individuals out of 12 who went to explore the land of Canaan lived durably and enjoyed the fruit of stick-to-it-iveness.

••

Read Numbers 13:27–14:10, and identify what set Joshua and Caleb apart from the ten other spies who acted so fearful and disgruntled.

The Apostle Paul assists us in understanding how to live content. *Read Philippians 4:10–13,* and answer the following questions.

What is the significance of Paul stating the he "learned" to live content?

What was Paul's secret to living content?

Are there any areas of your life in which you are currently struggling to be content? Take a moment to identify these challenging areas. Will you surrender them to God in prayer?

••

Day 6
Choose Joy

The final action for finishing well is choosing joy. Paul wrote, "But even if I am being poured out like a drink offering on the sacrifice and service coming from your faith, I am glad and rejoice with all of you. So you too should be glad and rejoice with me" (Philippians 2:17–18).

Here, Paul commands the church to join him in being joyful while he sits in a prison cell. Does this seem strange?

In Philippians 1, Paul presents three snapshots of choosing joy. *Read the following passages,* and identify three reasons he chose joy.

Philippians 1:12–14

Philippians 1:15–18

Philippians 1:21–26

As it did for Nehemiah, the joy of the Lord became Paul's strength (Nehemiah 8:10). Paul never reflected a "woe is me" mentality in life or ministry. Although he wrote this letter from a prison cell and his fate remained uncertain, he rose above his circumstances and chose joy. In his sermon, "The Epistle of Joy," pastor John MacArthur reminds us that the verb "to rejoice" appears 74 times in the New Testament and the noun "joy" appears 59 times in the New Testament and 16 times in this letter to the Philippians. The sheer volume of use throughout the New Testament suggests that joy is an attribute to be pursued through Christ.

Choosing joy allows us to rise above the most challenging circumstances in our lives in our pursuit of finishing well. Paul experienced his fair share of Heartbreak Hills, but he kept running with great joy (2 Corinthians 12:7–10). Paul could not change his environment, but he could control his disposition by living joyfully. Twice in this passage, Paul commanded the church to be glad and rejoice with him. His attitude of joy enabled him to persevere and finish well. In his article, "Choosing Joy," from the *Discipleship Journal*, Mark Reed provides some helpful counsel regarding our privilege to choose joy:

> Joy is a choice made by those who discipline their attitudes. Joy is not automatic. It doesn't seize you and force you under its will like a sovereign hand. You don't catch it like a virus. It is work. Happiness stems from what happens; it is a feeling that surges and fades. Joy, on the other hand, stems from the Holy Spirit, and can be a constant regardless of circumstances.

The Apostle Paul reminds us that the world has the potential to beat us up, and we need God's Spirit to prompt in us the fruitful disposition of joy. Let's face it: life does not play out with sweet sentiments like a Hallmark commercial. Nope, in real life we have financial worries, relational problems, physical challenges, emotional stress, and a slew of seemingly insurmountable obstacles facing us. But Paul says regardless of your Heartbreak Hill, you can always work for joy and therefore finish well.

Coach Tony Dungy epitomizes how the firing of the clay produces spiritual endurance. In 2001, when the Tampa Bay Buccaneers fired him as head coach for not winning the Super Bowl, Tony Dungy experienced the extreme heat of the Potter's kiln. Dungy said of the ordeal, "It was one of the biggest disappointments in my life because I did feel like the Lord had brought me down to Tampa." As Dungy tried to discern God's will for his future, he received a call from Jim Irsay, the owner of the Indianapolis Colts. God opened the door, and in 2002 the Colts hired him to lead their team, which he did, all the way to a Super Bowl championship in 2007 by defeating the Chicago Bears 29–17.

However, the road to glory included another fiery furnace for Dungy to experience. On December 22, 2005, his son James committed suicide at the age of 18. This loss took place a few weeks before the American Football Conference (AFC) division playoff against the Pittsburg Steelers. Although the Colts lost to the Steelers, Dungy showed up and led his team well, once again demonstrating the resilience that comes through faith in Christ.

The pain of those experiences was enormous, but today Dungy looks back and provides clarity and wisdom for the road ahead.

Life is challenging. I wish I could tell you that you'll always be on top of the mountain, but the reality is that there are days when nothing will go right, when not only will you not be on top, you may not even be able to figure out which way is up. Do yourself a favor, and don't make it any harder than it has to be. In those moments, be careful how you speak to yourself; be careful how you think of yourself; be careful how you conduct yourself; be careful how you develop yourself.

Tony Dungy epitomizes what it looks like to never give up and finish well. His life inspires us to fight the good fight, to finish the course, and to keep the faith (2 Timothy 4:7). Henry Wadsworth Longfellow said, "Great is that art of beginning but greater is the art of ending."

Father,
Thank You for creating me to live durably and
finish well. Lord, I confess that in order to finish well,
some changes must take place in my life. Renew in me
a commitment to do my part, knowing that You are
faithful to do Yours. Help me to yield as humble,
content, and joyful clay in Your faithful hands.
In Jesus' name, I pray.
Amen.

spiritual inventory

Do you view your faith journey as a long obedience in the same direction?

_____

_____

_____

Are you currently pressing on to the high calling of God in Christ Jesus (Philippians 3:14)? _____

_____

_____

Do you value the temperature of the kiln as it heats up to transform your clay pot into a durable and immortal vessel? _____

_____

_____

_____

Do the glazes of humility, contentment, and joy beautify the piece that God is currently firing? _____

_____

_____

_____

Will you continue to fix your eyes on Jesus, who relentlessly works in you to will and to act according to His good purpose? _____

_____

_____

_____

How is your today going to impact your tomorrow and the goal of finishing well? _____

_____

_____

_____

WEEK 7

TREASURE: *Hope for the Hurting*

2 CORINTHIANS 4:7

*My deepest awareness of myself is that
I am deeply loved by Jesus Christ and I have done
nothing to earn it or deserve it.*
—Brennan Manning

Day 1
The Gospel

Scholars have hailed the discovery of the Dead Sea Scrolls as the greatest literary and archaeological discovery of our time. Between the years of 1947 and 1956, some 931 documents were discovered in 11 caves along the northwestern shore of the Dead Sea in southern Israel. These manuscripts include both biblical and non-biblical material, including fragments from every book of the Hebrew Old Testament except the Book of Esther. Written predominantly in Hebrew and Aramaic, the scrolls appear to be the library of a Jewish sect known as the Essenes, who lived in the Qumran community from around 200 BC to AD 68.

One manuscript, known as the Isaiah Scroll, is 1,000 years older than its principal Masoretic text. The Masoretes were a group of scribe-scholars that lived between the sixth and tenth centuries who labored to preserve the text of the Hebrew Old Testament Scriptures.

The Masoretic text is used in all modern translations, and it bears a remarkable agreement with the earlier document. These ancient texts have greatly enriched our understanding of both Judaism and Christianity, allowing comparative religious studies. Ironically, this priceless treasure chest from antiquity that has enhanced biblical studies was housed and preserved in ordinary clay pots for more than 2,000 years.

These invaluable and irreplaceable manuscripts have a remarkable parallel in Paul's writing to the Corinthian church when he wrote, "But we have this treasure in jars of clay to show that this all-surpassing power is from God and not from us" (2 Corinthians 4:7). The treasure Paul speaks of is God's Word and message embodied in the gospel of Jesus Christ. The Spirit of God is the one who deposits the gospel in all clay vessels who know Jesus personally.

••

Read the following passages of Scripture, and record all the terms you find that describe the treasure of God's Word.

Isaiah 40:8

Psalm 19:7–8

Acts 20:24

Romans 1:16–17

Hebrews 4:12

List the ultimate reason the Apostle Paul gave to never be ashamed of the gospel treasure.

According to Hebrews, how confident should we be in the effectiveness of the gospel?

••

According to these verses and many others, the container may be common, but the contents are supernatural. Do you see the irony regarding this treasure? Typically, people put valuables in protective environments, like safes, bank vaults, or safe deposit boxes, where the treasures are secure or even insured. However, God puts His prized possession of the gospel in everyday, ordinary containers of clay, like you and me. In the first century, pots of clay were as common as Tupperware is today and could be seen everywhere—from homes to marketplaces. They stored everything, including water, food, fuel, and the family valuables.

In this passage, the Apostle Paul makes a striking contrast between the incomparable and the common. Once again the metaphor of clay provides great clarity in establishing biblical ideals for the people of God to live in a way useful to the Master.

spiritual inventory

What truth captured your heart most in this lesson?_____

_____

_____

_____

_____

Are you comfortable sharing the gospel with others?_____

_____

_____

_____

_____

Is there anyone in your sphere of influence that needs the treasure of the gospel that you can pray for and begin building a relational bridge toward?_____

_____

_____

_____

_____

_____

_____

_____

Day 2
We

Knowing that God deposits His treasure in jars of clay should inspire us to live in a manner worthy of the gospel. Look again at 2 Corinthians 4:7 (HCSB), "Now we have this treasure in clay jars, so that this extraordinary power may be from God and not from us," and consider three inspiring spiritual realities over the next few days.

The first reality reminds followers of Christ that we are the hope of the world. When Paul says "we" have this treasure, he is not just referring to himself or his colleagues in ministry, but to all who are "in Christ" (Ephesians 1:13–14). Jesus modeled a team approach to ministry (Luke 10:1–2) and then commanded His followers to go into all the world and make disciples (Matthew 28:16–20). He gave us His Holy Spirit for empowerment and promised that "we" would be His witnesses, starting at home and extending our reach to the ends of the earth (Acts 1:8). With more than 7 billion people populating planet Earth, that directive might sound like "mission impossible." However, I would contend if all do their part, the task seems much more reasonable and accomplishable. It should be obvious that the gospel advances best when each member of the body of Christ does his or her part.

•••

Write out Ephesians 4:16.

What kind of impact do you think it would have on the kingdom of God if every believer was doing his or her part in ministry?

•••

A marvelous picture of each member doing his or her part comes from the near-tragedy of the Apollo 13 mission. On April 11, 1970, the National Aeronautics and Space Administration (NASA) launched the three-man crew of John Swigert, Fred Haise, and James Lovell into space. Their purpose involved numerous experiments, obtaining lunar samples, and unique photographic assignments. The mission launched well as early reports from NASA confirm.

During the first two days, the crew ran into a couple of minor surprises, but generally Apollo 13 was looking like the smoothest flight of the program. At 46 hours, 43 minutes Joe Kerwin, the capsule communicator, or capcom, on duty, said, "The spacecraft is in real good shape as far as we are concerned. We're bored to tears down here."

However, on April 13, shortly after the crew finished a 49-minute television broadcast showing how comfortably they lived and worked in weightlessness, an in-flight explosion crippled the spacecraft. Command module pilot John Swigert uttered the words, "Houston, we've had a problem," which are now infamous in space history.

If you have seen the movie *Apollo 13*, starring Tom Hanks, you may remember the scene where NASA engineers and scientists gathered together to assess the situation and explore every possible means and resource available to get the three astronauts home. Mission control created an "all hands on deck" approach and worked in concert with the astronauts to accomplish mission impossible. On April 17—five days, 22 hours, and 54 minutes into the mission—Apollo 13 gently splashed down into the Pacific Ocean near Samoa, with the USS *Iwo Jima* assisting in the rescue.

Mission control of Apollo 13 reminds the church of the paradigm that Christ chose to take the treasure of the gospel to the ends of the earth. The body of Christ must function more like NASA in our kingdom assignments. Christ always intended our missions efforts to reflect an "all hands on deck" mentality. We need to view our efforts as complementary in the body of Christ and work in concert, using every resource and means available to be the light of the world and salt of the earth.

A few times a year, I have the privilege of leading missions teams to Africa. Most teams are no larger than a handful of people. However, dozens participate in these missions endeavors through prayer, financial support, and encouragement to the families while the team is away. It costs about $20,000 to send a team of six to Africa. That means roughly 150 to 200 financial supporters. Recently, one family contributed $3,000 to purchase solar-powered audio Bibles so the Bambara people could hear the gospel in their native tongue. A generous businessman in our church funded the construction of a home so we could live among the people. Another donor provided $10,000 to be used at our discretion for ministry expenses. A gentleman who owns a tool store donated two generators so we could show the *Jesus* film. For every one team member going to Mali, there are dozens who come alongside in unique and complementary ways.

· ·

Write out Mark 6:7, and describe how Jesus sent out His disciples for kingdom efforts.

The early church commissioned and supported team ministry. See if you can supply the unique team member:

Barnabas and _____ (Acts 13:1–5)

Paul and _____ (Acts 15:39–40)

Barnabas and _____ (Acts 15:39–40)

Silas and _____ (Acts 17:13–15)

Paul, Priscilla, and _____ (Acts 18:18)

Priscilla, Aquila, and _____ (Acts 18:24–28)

Timothy and _____ (Acts 19:21–22)

· ·

Luke portrays team ministry as normative in the Book of Acts. The gospel advanced throughout the Mediterranean world, as these teams banded together and turned the world upside down for the gospel. While writing this chapter, I received an email from one of our church secretaries that accents the value of doing ministry together:

> Hi team,
> I just received a call from a gal named Marilyn. She lives in Prior Lake and asked what time our Good Friday service was. She said she wanted to come because one day a couple [from Friendship Church] stopped at her door to welcome her and give her a [local coffee shop] gift card. She told them that she had breast cancer and now she has brain cancer. She is coming [to church this weekend] with her two adult children. I mentioned the [Good Friday] prayerwalk, and she said she definitely wants to do that, too. Be encouraged. Thanks for all you do to speak truth to our community and beyond. I'll get back to work now, as soon as the tears quit forming in my eyes. I am blessed to answer calls at the Welcome Center.

What a marvelous picture of God watering seeds that were planted many months prior by servants who said yes to going door to door and welcoming new families into our community.

••

Are you currently involved in a ministry team that prioritizes sharing the good news of Jesus Christ?

••

Day 3
Treasure

The second reality from 2 Corinthians 4:7 reminds Christians that the gospel is the hope of the world. Occasionally, clay pots were used in the ancient world as safety deposit boxes. These vaults would contain valuables like gold, silver, and jewelry. The Greek historian Plutarch described the celebration of the Macedonian victory of Aemilius Paulus in 167 BC and how 3,000 men carried away the spoil of silver coins in 750 clay pots. Paul uses the Greek word *thesaurus* to promote the exceptional value of the treasure deposited in jars of clay. In Matthew 13:44–46 Jesus used the same term and likened the kingdom of God to finding priceless treasure. At times, these treasure chests were buried in the ground, only to be discovered by some random traveler. Of course, the invaluable treasure that Paul speaks of is the gospel of Jesus Christ.

From a human vantage point, it seems nonsensical to place such irreplaceable treasure like the gospel in ordinary vessels like you and me—unless of course, you want to magnify the treasure and not the container. That is exactly what Scripture teaches. According to Paul, the powerful gospel "is from God and not from us" (2 Corinthians 4:7).

Write out Matthew 13:44–46.

According to Christ, because this treasure is more valuable than anything we could possibly pursue or possess, it is worth every sacrifice and commitment to obtain it. Notice how willingly both individuals gave up everything they owned to acquire the gift of God, which is eternal life through Jesus Christ our Lord (Romans 6:23).

Recently, a gentleman new to our church told me that after a Sunday morning worship service, he could not get the gospel message out of his mind. The next morning, while he was driving to work, the Spirit of God convicted him of sin, and with a repentant heart he cried out to the Lord for salvation. He told me that tears of joy overwhelmed him as he declared, "I'm all in, Lord." He testified that since then he has "never been so contented in his life." That transformation can only happen when the Spirit of God takes the treasure of God and causes broken individuals like my friend to relinquish all and acquire the glorious gift of salvation through Jesus Christ our Lord.

Erich Bridges and Jerry Rankin authored an inspirational book titled *Lives Given, Not Taken: 21st Century Southern Baptist Martyrs*. Their anthology of eight modern missionaries who went to "dangerous places" testifies of the greatness of the treasure we have in jars of clay. They tell the story of Karen Watson, who was commissioned by the International Mission Board to serve in Iraq. Her role involved coordinating postwar relief projects in the name of Christ.

The authors never personally met Watson; however, they got to know her through an exhaustive reading of her memoirs. They wrote candidly about her clay pot experiences, suggesting that Karen had a "tough childhood" and "a lot of hurt." They describe Watson's devastating losses of loved ones, her battle with anger, depression, and loneliness, and years of emotional pain, all of which she freely shared with others. However, when Watson embraced the treasure of the gospel, she became a bold and joyful servant of the Lord. Before leaving for Iraq, she wrote a letter. Phil Neighbors, one of her pastors at Valley Baptist Church in Bakersfield, California, later discovered it. The envelope was sealed and labeled, "Open in case of death." A little more than a year into her tour of ministry, Karen and three missionary colleagues were killed by anonymous gunmen. This love letter, written to her family, church, and God, expresses her passion because of the treasure deposited in her at salvation:

> Dear Pastor Phil and Pastor Roger,
> You should only be opening this in the event of death. When God calls there are no regrets. I tried to share my heart with you as much as possible, my heart for the nations. I wasn't called to a place; I was called to Him. To obey was my objective, to suffer was expected, His glory my reward, His glory my reward . . .
>
> The missionary heart:
> Cares more than some think is wise
> Risks more than some think is safe
> Dreams more than some think is practical

Expects more than some think is possible

I was called not to comfort or success but to obedience . . .

There is no joy outside of knowing Jesus and serving Him. I love you two and my church family.

In His care,

Salaam, Karen

Karen Watson embodied what it means for us to possess His treasure in our jars of clay. The riches of the glorious gospel transformed her broken clay vessel, which resulted in her living a life to the glory of God. She magnified the contents of the vessel by putting God on display in all she did, including her death. Karen's legacy reminds us that the all-surpassing power of the gospel is from God and not from us.

•••

Take a few moments and let Karen's story inspire a written prayer that is personal to you and the Lord.

•••

Day 4
Jars of Clay

The final reality from 2 Corinthians 4:7 reminds genuine believers that in our weaknesses we bring hope to the world. J. T. Fitzgerald suggests, "an earthen vessel is 'quintessentially fragile,' prone to breakage, easily chipped and cracked." I am convinced Paul used this metaphor intentionally to underscore his weakness and frailty as a clay vessel. By his own admission, he was timid (2 Corinthians 10:1) and lacked communication skills (11:6). Paul's critics agreed with his humble assessment. The Corinthians said, "His letters are weighty and forceful, but in person he is unimpressive and his speaking amounts to nothing" (10:10). He prayed much about his "thorn in the flesh," which, humanly speaking, could frustrate the advance of the gospel. However, Paul learned and then promoted weakness as a necessary strength for gospel ministry. He developed his theology of strength in weakness at the tail end of his second epistle to the Corinthian church.

....

Read 2 Corinthians 12:7–10. Why did God choose to let Paul's thorn in the flesh prevail?

Read 2 Corinthians 13:4. Where did Paul get this paradoxical idea that strength comes through weakness?

....

Paul's personal testimony emulated the life and ministry of his Savior. As a result, Paul boasted and delighted in his weakness so that the treasure contained in his clay vessel could become most prominent. Because Paul never wanted to become the center of attention and shortchange the gospel, he embraced the God-honoring disposition of humility. According to 2 Corinthians 12:1-6, Paul had experiences with God that few others could boast about. He describes being taken up into the third heaven, where God dwells, and receiving surpassingly great revelations from the Lord. Just imagine the impact of such an experience. Clearly, Paul could have set himself above the other apostles or become conceited about his spiritual encounters and accomplishments. However,

Paul recognized God had ordained his thorn in the flesh to prevent pride and promote weakness and humility in his life. If we are honest, given the opportunity, most of us would enjoy displaying our spiritual resumes and being honored for our achievements. We struggle to embrace the disposition of Paul, who wanted to decrease so the gospel of Christ might increase. But, Scripture is clear that God shapes our clay pots with weakness and humility to properly exhibit His treasure. William Booth, the founder of The Salvation Army, prioritized these attributes of weakness and humility for every member who served in his organization. In 1878, as Booth's ministry began making its mark for Christ's kingdom, men and women started enlisting from all over the world. The famed Samuel Brengle left behind a fine pastorate in America and crossed the Atlantic to join Booth's Army.

At first General Booth accepted his services reluctantly and grudgingly. Booth said to Brengle, "You've been your own boss too long." So in order to instill humility in Brengle, he set him to work cleaning the boots of other trainees. Discouraged, Brengle said to himself, "Have I followed my own fancy across the Atlantic in order to black boots?" And then, as if in a vision, he saw Jesus bending over the feet of rough fishermen. "Lord," he whispered, "you washed their feet; I will black their shoes."

Weakness and humility laid the foundation for Samuel Brengle's ministry in the Army. Consequently, God's servant rose through the ranks and attained the status of commissioner, becoming the first American-born officer to reach that status in The Salvation Army. Our jars of clay constantly remind us that God is not interested in sanctified celebrities, because there are no Grammy Awards for our kingdom assignments.

....

What do you sense God saying to you about any "apparent" weaknesses in your life?

Are you ready to embrace your weaknesses like Paul did as an opportunity to experience grace and power for ministry?

....

Day 5
Weakness and Humility

These attributes of weakness and humility fly in the face of our so-called Christian cultural values, expressed so poignantly through the cliché, "God helps those who help themselves." A Gallup poll reported that 82 percent of Americans think this cliché is actually a Bible verse. Of course, this platitude is not found in the Bible, and it actually conflicts with the foundational truths of Christianity. So, Paul provided clarity by presenting the reason for this stark contrast of the gospel, reminding us that God's power in our lives is perfected in times of weakness. That means our weakness and God's strength exist simultaneously, because according to James Dunn in his book *Jesus and the Spirit* "power does not drive out weakness; on the contrary, it only comes to its full strength in and through weakness" (see 2 Corinthians 12:9). Paul wanted the church to realize that we are most powerful when we rely least on our own resources and strength.

Strength through weakness is the reason God commanded Gideon to strip his army down from 32,000 men to 300 before he fought the Midianites (Judges 7:2–8). The story of Esther champions this principle, as God worked powerfully through a teenager to rescue the Hebrew nation from genocide in 127 provinces of Persia.

A old seminary instructor once told the story of a Polish man who was enslaved by Nazis during World War II and forced to work in an armaments factory. He wanted to help free his countrymen, but each day he was told that if he didn't work, his family would be killed. On a reconnaissance flight over Germany, a British spy plane was pursued by a German fighter plane. The German fighter plane shot 50 accurate rounds of combustion bullets into the fuselage of the British plane, but none of the bullets exploded. The British pilot made it back safely with valuable aerial photographs. When his plane was inspected, the bullets were pulled from the fuselage and were found to contain no powder. Inside one bullet was a note from the Polish armaments worker. In his language it said, "I'm sorry. This is all I can do for now." After the photos were developed, a successful air raid was launched against a German garrison. The Polish worker never knew that his "weak contribution" had been providentially responsible for felling a large arsenal. This extraordinary story is reminiscent of Kittie L. Suffield's hymn, "Little Is Much When God Is in It." Humility, coupled with our weakness, provides the platform for the Lord to demonstrate His glory and goodness.

In 537 BC, God called Zerubbabel to the monumental task of rebuilding the Temple in Jerusalem. This building project would launch the spiritual renewal of God's people as they returned from Babylonian captivity. However, opposition to God's work resulted in Zerubbabel feeling inadequate and abandoning the reconstruction for 15 years (Ezra 4:24). So, God renewed Zerubbabel's kingdom assignment and communicated how it could only be accomplished by His Spirit's sovereign and powerful work in and through His servants.

••

Write out Zechariah 4:6.

Outline how God manifested His power through the following individuals' weak and frail circumstances:

David (1 Samuel 17:1–9; 32–51)

Elizabeth and Zechariah (Luke 1:5–25)

••

The humble evangelist Billy Graham understood this truth when he declared, "If God should take His hands off my life, my lips would turn to clay." Like Paul, Graham could boast in his accomplishments for Christ's kingdom. In the twentieth century, his preaching ministry exposed millions to the gospel of Jesus Christ, with thousands making genuine faith commitments. Graham understood the contrasting relationship between his weakness and God's power. He knew the treasured gospel is best communicated through a frail, dependent, and humble spirit that totally relies on God. St. Francis of Assisi is one of the most venerated religious figures in history. When asked how he was able accomplish so much for the Lord, he replied:

> This may be why: The Lord looked down from heaven and said, "Where can I find the weakest, littlest man on earth?" Then He saw me and said, "I've found him. I will work through him, and he won't be proud of it. He'll see that I am only using him because of his insignificance."

Assisi captures the heart of the Apostle Paul and the true meaning behind the metaphor of God using weak, fragile, and broken pots for His glory. A. W. Tozer presents a worthwhile reminder: "I think it may be safely said that God is still looking for men who know their own insufficiencies so well that He can perform the miraculous through them."

How is God using your apparent weakness to strengthen you for ministry?

Day 6
Leading with a Limp—My Story

••••••••••••••••••••••••••••••••••••••

Have you ever felt inadequate for ministry?

Have you ever looked in the mirror and said, "Lord, I wish you would have made me different?"

Have you ever compared yourself to others and thought, "I'm not as gifted as he or she is" or "I wish I had the talent of that guy"?

••••••••••••••••••••••••••••••••••••••

The Spirit of God dealt with some of my inadequacies in the fall of 2012, when I spent a few days enjoying the Crossing Borders art tour throughout the North Shore in Minnesota. Our church was experiencing some unusual challenges in ministry, and as lead pastor I personally felt discouraged. Times like this can emphasize our imperfections and feelings of incompetence. Satan has a calculated way of magnifying our cracks and flaws, reminding us how weak and frail we really are. However, God intervened and led me to *KKD Pottery* in Grand Marais, Minnesota. That day, potter Kristi Downing was hosting a Raku firing. During a period of five hours, Kristi demonstrated the art of shaping raw clay, bisque firing, glazing, gas firing, then using combustibles to bring about a spontaneous and unpredictable beauty in the finished products. At one point in the demonstration, Kristi had a piece that "fell off" in the bisque firing stage. Instead of discarding the clay, she decided to see it to completion. I jokingly said to Kristy, "That vase reflects my life and ministry more than any other piece in your studio."

"How so?" she inquired.

"The broken piece reminds me that I have always led with a limp," I responded. With iron tongs, Kristy retrieved that red hot Raku piece from a container filled with combustibles. After cooling it in water, she began scrubbing it feverishly. Within seconds the beauty within the clay began to manifest itself. Kristy named the jar "leading with a limp" and presented it to me as a gift. Today, it sits on my roll top desk in my home office. It is a beautiful reminder of how God uses clay pots that are broken, humble, and limp. I want to challenge you to join me in learning a valuable lesson. Our ordinary vessels do not have to hinder His powerful gospel from working in and through us. Could it be that our flaws, chips, and cracks allow His glorious gospel to shine even brighter? I think Christian artist Jason Gray would offer a resounding "yea and amen" to that proposition. A few years ago, he did a concert in our church and informed us that God had blessed him with the gift of stuttering. I sensed, in that moment, our learning of his handicap endeared the audience to him. When he sang, all stuttering ceased, as the Spirit's power became more evident through his limitations.

••

Have you ever stopped to consider that maybe your weaknesses are His greatest strength—allowing others to see Christ more visibly in you and be drawn to Him in greater ways?

Could it be that today, for the first time in your spiritual journey, you would bow your head and thank God for the weaknesses you possess that allow His strength to be realized?

••

God's Glory and the Game of Golf

I want to conclude this chapter by letting an old friend, Wendel Deyo, the national director of Athletes in Action, remind us how God uses our clay vessels and cracked pots for His glory. For those of you, like me, who aspire to a better game of golf, you will truly appreciate this story.

> Nine holes. It began, innocently enough, as a way for Cindy and me to spend the morning together. I wished we'd stopped after eight. A poor shot off of the ninth tee put me just off to the right of Cindy. And since the ninth fairway was still 500 yards away, I opted to pull out the old two iron and let it rip. One principle in golf is never to swing hard. Another should be, don't broadcast it when you do.
>
> Swinging as hard as I could, in my backswing I yelled to Cindy, "Watch this, sweetheart!" Just as she turned her head toward my arrogant remark, the ball hit her sharply in the upper corner of her right eye below the eyebrow. Cindy fell flat on her face. Praying immediately, and sprinting to her aid, I rolled her over, pulling her hands from her face to see the gash split open to the orbital and gushing with blood.

We prayed for her sight, for help, for supernatural healing, for God's grace, for everything that flashed across our minds. After putting my handkerchief over the wound, I ran through the woods, jumped the creek and out into the first fairway. Just as a golfer was putting a club into his bag, I stole his cart, explaining as I pulled away that I needed it worse than he! Taking the shortcut through the creek as well as the woods, I loaded Cindy in the cart and sped toward the car. As we raced for the hospital, Cindy prayed for our children and other selfless requests as I prayed for her. As we entered the emergency room of Bethesda North Hospital, the attending physician immediately and wisely sent us to the Cincinnati Eye Institute. It just "happened" to be next door.

Five doctors later, Cindy was ready to be admitted to the hospital. After plastic surgery, a medical assistant wheeled Cindy back to the hospital. As I trailed behind Cindy in the wheelchair, I reflected on the previous hours, God's grace, and my errant swing. It was humbling. I remembered Dr. Bright once saying "the best way to be humble is to be humiliated." I was.

But the best was yet to come. Cindy had not been able to open either eye since the accident, and now both eyes were covered by a head wrapping. As I was finalizing the hospital admittance procedure, I stepped out of the office to ask Cindy her social security number and witnessed an even more humbling sight. Never having seen the medical assistant and still not sure she would see out of her right eye again, Cindy was sharing Christ with her! Witnessing was one of the farthest things from my mind.

Throughout her stay in the hospital, Cindy witnessed to nurses like Paul witnessed to prison guards, with shift changes seen as new witness opportunities. As she checked out of the hospital, she sent some of her flowers with a four spiritual laws booklet to the man next door. Minutes later, a nurse came in to thank Cindy. As tears rolled down her cheek she said, "The man you gave the flowers to is my father-in-law. He had no flowers. He's dying. I just wanted to thank you for being so thoughtful." I remain humbled, marveling at God's grace and Cindy's faithfulness to share her faith. The medical assistant is now a sister in Christ, and Cindy is meeting with her one-on-one. My golf game is still lousy, but God's sovereignty is not.

The next time you pick up a golf ball, take a close look at it and let it remind you of God's strength in your weakness.

In her frailty, Cindy Deyo let the priceless treasure of the glorious gospel shine through her. God's power was perfected in her absolute weakness. Oswald Chambers ties this truth together, stating:

God can achieve his purpose either through the absence of human power and resources, or the abandonment of reliance on them. All through history God has chosen and used nobodies, because the unusual dependence on him made possible the unique display of his power and grace. He chose and used somebodies only when they renounced dependence on their natural abilities and resources.

May we, like Paul and many of God's faithful servants, embrace our weaknesses so others may discover the treasure of the gospel!

Father,
Thank You for depositing Your treasured gospel
in my clay vessel. I confess, Lord, I have not always been
faithful to declare Your glorious grace. Give me courage to
embrace my weaknesses so Your power can be displayed
in and through me. I long to do my part and ask that
You lead me to discover how I best can serve to advance
Your glorious gospel. In Jesus' name, I pray.
Amen.

WEEK 8

SOVEREIGNTY:
Trusting God When Life Does Not Make Sense

ISAIAH 45:9

*What an incredible witness it is to a lost and fearful
society when the Christian acts like a child of God, living under
the loving sovereignty of the Heavenly Father.*
—Henry Blackaby

Day 1
Wonderfully Sovereign

In 1967, at age 17, Joni Eareckson Tada was paralyzed from the shoulders down as the result of a diving accident. She struggled, as any person would, with doubt, frustration, and the sovereignty of God. However, God's grace prevailed over bitterness and hopelessness. In time, she learned to embrace her unique experience and honored the Potter by launching a ministry for the disabled, which has touched millions of lives for many decades. Through her broken vessel, the Master Potter provided a platform for Joni to address two of the most difficult topics in life: our suffering and God's sovereignty. In a pamphlet she wrote titled, *Is God Really in Control?*, she declares,

> Nothing is a surprise to God, nothing is a setback to his plans; nothing can thwart his purposes; and nothing is beyond his control. His sovereignty is absolute. Everything that happens is uniquely ordained of God. Sovereignty is a weighty thing to ascribe to the nature and character of God. Yet if He were not sovereign, He would not be God. The Bible is clear that God is in control of everything that happens.

Years later, Joni was diagnosed with stage-two breast cancer and has suffered with chronic pain. She continued reflecting on suffering and sovereignty and released a sequel asking these same difficult questions. Her book, *A Place of Healing: Wrestling with the Mysteries of Suffering, Pain, and God's Sovereignty* once again clarifies how a sovereign God can allow suffering. In the final chapter, "Thank You, God, for this Wheelchair," Joni summarizes her deepest and most personal convictions regarding lifelong suffering. She describes how, over the years, many people tried to persuade her that the accident "was never part of God's plan" or that her paralysis and chronic pain "didn't have to be." However, Joni pushes back, saying, "I know differently," because she believes her loving and sovereign Potter "allowed" and "permitted" her handicap for the good of others and the glory of her Savior. After numerous decades of severe and escalating suffering, Joni continues to find strength in the Lord, concluding that healing and wholeness in the midst of pain and hardship come from resting in "our wonderfully sovereign God."

Joni's strong conviction of the sovereignty of God is deeply rooted in Scripture.

··

Choose two or three of the following passages and describe how these individuals embraced the Potter's sovereign hand in their lives.

Genesis 6:11–22

2 Samuel 7:18–29

Daniel 1:1–21

Luke 2:25–35

Acts 4:23–31

··

Choosing the clay and what the terra-cotta becomes is the potter's prerogative. The potter stands sovereign over the clay and, out of love, shapes it according to his vision and purpose. For many individuals, including some Christians, that proposition is a hard pill to swallow. Most people have no problem embracing the rule of God when things are going well. However, how do we respond when life gets turned upside down? Do we believe the Potter is really in control?

··

How did you react the last time you faced a financial hardship, a broken relationship, the loss of a job or home, or the hurt of a wayward child? Did you trust God during those difficult times?

Did you experience His tender, loving care? Was He still on the throne of your life?

··

Now, take the introspection a step further. Some of you have dealt with the wounds of abuse, abandonment, infidelity, or divorce. You were blindsided by a terminal disease or the tragic loss a loved one. You can more readily identify with individuals such as Joni Eareckson Tada. You are no stranger to the Job-like trials of life. My guess is that during those times you struggled to comprehend and embrace God's sovereign rule in your life. You have more questions than you do answers. Theologian R. C. Sproul speaks to this tension:

> I have never in my life met a Christian who said that he did not believe that God is sovereign . . . but as soon as we probe the understanding of sovereignty, it takes about five minutes to realize that how many Christians define sovereignty could be better described as non-sovereignty . . . a God who is like the king of England, who reigns but does not rule.

No Christian is exempt from the temptation to relegate God's sovereignty to a more passive oversight of His creation. Therefore, we must work hard to trust Him even when the storms of life are raging and it makes little sense.

In his youth, David embodied this disposition of believing that God is in control. While Saul and the armies of Israel stood paralyzed by the Philistine militia and the giant Goliath (1 Samuel 17), David put his hope in Almighty God. The young shepherd reminds us to "look back" in order to "move forward" regardless of the situation. David persuaded Saul to let him fight the uncircumcised warrior by telling the king a "God story." David reminisced about how the living God delivered him from "the paw of the lion and the paw of the bear" (v. 37). David challenges us to look in the rearview mirror with eyes of faith and be reminded of the powerful presence of God.

Are you currently struggling to trust God like King Saul and the armies of Israel? If so, I want to encourage you to be like David and "remember the deeds of the LORD" (Psalm 77:11). Cling to the truth that "Jesus Christ is the same yesterday and today and forever" (Hebrews 13:8). Never forget that God's fidelity is tied to His character and "he remains faithful, for he cannot disown himself" (2 Timothy 2:13).

••

Is R. C. Sproul right? Does the average Christian have such a limited understanding of the sovereignty of God?

When was the last time the sovereignty of God was made real in your life? What happened and how did you respond? Did you trust the Lord or did you begin to backpedal and wonder if God was really in control?

••

Day 2
Ruling and Overruling

Centuries ago, God addressed our ongoing dilemma to appropriate His sovereign rule in our lives. He longs for us to realize that He is on the throne, ruling and overruling, even when life does not make sense. In 586 BC, Nebuchadnezzar devastated the city of Jerusalem, which included destroying the temple of God and carrying many captives into exile. However, because God sees the end from the beginning, He forecasted the ascendancy of a pagan king named Cyrus a century before Cyrus's birth, who would do His will at the appointed time (Jeremiah 29:10). In divine providence God orchestrated the founding of the Persian Empire through Cyrus as he assumed rule in Eastern Elam in 559 BC. His reign expanded a decade later when he conquered the Medes and unified the Medo-Persian Empire. According to the prophet Daniel, God's plans expanded to include Babylon, which Cyrus subjugated in 539 BC (Daniel 5:20). To fulfill God's purposes, the very next year, Cyrus issued a decree that the Jews could return to Jerusalem and rebuild the Temple. These sovereign acts, accomplished across many decades, involved numerous world leaders and empires. They should remind us that God is seated on His throne, ruling and overruling. Ezra records God's supreme declaration:

> In the first year of Cyrus king of Persia, in order to fulfill the word of the LORD spoken by Jeremiah, the LORD moved the heart of Cyrus king of Persia to make a proclamation throughout his realm and to put it in writing: "This is what Cyrus king of Persia says: 'The LORD, the God of heaven, has given me all the kingdoms of the earth and he has appointed me to build a temple for him at Jerusalem in Judah. Any of his people among you may go up to Jerusalem in Judah and build the temple of the LORD, the God of Israel, the God who is in Jerusalem, and may their God be with them.'" —Ezra 1:1–3

According to Ezra, who was responsible for the king's decree to release the Jews to rebuild the Temple?

How did Cyrus view his God-ordained role as monarch?

Read Proverbs 21:1. How does this verse and God's interaction with King Cyrus support us in trusting the Lord when the global scene seems to be spinning out of control?

....

Did you notice that Ezra put the onus on God, who moved the heart of the king, to issue the decree? Humanly speaking, the destiny of God's people seemed to rest in the hands of the most powerful monarch of that day. However, Ezra declared that God was fulfilling His word spoken through the prophet Jeremiah (Jeremiah 25:12–14).

Another astonishing thing about God's choice is that Cyrus did not acknowledge the Lord (Isaiah 45:5). This sovereign decree that God would raise up a Gentile king to serve as a "Messiah" figure, to release Israel from their captivity, not only confounded Israel but frustrated them. So, the Potter takes action and brings clarity to Israel regarding His lordship:

> Woe to those who quarrel with their Maker, those who are nothing but potsherds among the potsherds on ground. Does the clay say to the potter, "What are you making?" Does your work say, "The potter has no hands?" —Isaiah 45:9

....

How does the metaphor of potter and clay assist us in understanding the sovereignty of God?

Have you ever found yourself "quarreling" with God as He shapes the clay of your life?

....

History records that the Jewish exiles did return and completed the Temple reconstruction around 520 BC. In addition, phase two of the rebuild came around 445 BC when Nehemiah returned to Jerusalem and rebuilt the city walls (Nehemiah 6:15). In her book *Grace Grows Best in Winter*, Margaret Clarkson masterfully depicts the rule of God in our lives:

> The sovereignty of God is the one impregnable rock to which the suffering human heart must cling. The circumstances surrounding our lives are no accident: they may be the work of evil, but that

evil is held firmly within the mighty hand of our sovereign God . . . . All evil is subject to Him, and evil cannot touch His children unless He permits it. God is the Lord of human history and of the personal history of every member of His redeemed family.

Decades of biblical studies and pastoral ministry has taught me many things, but the one reality that towers above all is that God has not relinquished His throne to another. He continues to rule and overrule. We must remember, "In the LORD's hand the king's heart is a stream of water that he channels toward all who please him" (Proverbs 21:1).

When in doubt go back to Calvary. Undoubtedly, the Crucifixion of Christ was the most evil and glorious act in all of history. Evil—because the sinless Son of God died a barbaric death at the hands of wicked people. Glorious—because "God's deliberate plan and foreknowledge" were realized at Golgotha (Acts 2:23).

The Cross of our Savior demonstrates that God is committed to accomplishing His kingdom purposes on earth, even at great expense to Himself. When we struggle like Israel to trust God we must remember that is He is on the throne and we are not.

We need to relax and stop quarreling with our Maker as we grow to trust His faithful handiwork. Like a father with a child, the Master Potter has our best interest in mind (Isaiah 64:8; Matthew 7:11). He sees the end from the beginning and acts in accordance with His good, acceptable, and perfect will (Romans 12:2). His perplexing choice to provide Israel's redemption through Cyrus, King of Persia, and offer salvation through the death of His Son by Roman Crucifixion should encourage us to always trust in the Lord with all our heart and lean not on our own understanding (Proverbs 3:5–6) because His divine purposes stand (Isaiah 46:1–13).

•••••••••••••••••••••••••••••••••••••••

Take time to write a prayer of thanksgiving to God for His sovereign reign in your life. Be specific on how He has ruled and overruled to insure His purposes and plans stand in your life.

•••••••••••••••••••••••••••••••••••••••

Day 3
Behind the Curtain

The great patriarch Joseph illustrated God's scrupulous work in our lives in a profound and marvelous way. The Bible tells us that Jacob loved Joseph, the youngest of 12 sons, more than his other children, resulting in sibling rivalry and their hatred of Joseph. To add fuel to the fire, one day Joseph had a dream, and when he interpreted the dream to his brothers "they hated him all the more" (Genesis 37:1–8). This led to Joseph's brothers ostracizing him and selling him to Ishmaelite traders, who in turn marketed Joseph on the slave block in Egypt (Genesis 37:36). Talk about a dysfunctional family. The daytime talk show hosts would have had a field day with his story.

Like any young lad, Joseph dreamed of growing up in a healthy, loving, and caring environment. However, God had a different path for Joseph to follow. While in Egypt, Joseph's career flourished; he oversaw the whole household of Potiphar, who served Pharaoh as the captain of the guard (Genesis 39:4). But, Potiphar bought into a lie regarding Joseph and had him incarcerated. While in prison, "the LORD was with him; he showed him kindness and granted him favor in the eyes of the prison warden" (39:21). However, more than two years passed, and it looked as if the many injustices Joseph experienced would have the last word (41:1).

Try putting yourself in Joseph's shoes. While growing up in a large family, you do your best to honor God. However, in His divine wisdom, He chooses to interrupt core areas of your life, including family, future, and friends. Joseph could have believed his doubts and doubted his beliefs, but that never happened. Joseph's story does not end in jail.

....

Read Genesis 39:2 and 21, and describe God's relationship with Joseph during these troubling times.

These verses remind us that God never leaves us or forsakes us, and the Grand Weaver divinely orchestrated one circumstance after another to accomplish His glorious will.

Write out Genesis 50:19–20.

How did God's providential work impact how he dealt with his painful situation?

....

In the end, Joseph became second-in-command for all of Egypt and concluded that God choreographed every aspect of his life for "the saving of many lives" (Genesis 50:20). In his book, *Is God Really in Control? Trusting God in a World of Hurt*, Jerry Bridges writes,

> **To believe in the sovereignty of God when we do not see His direct intervention—when God is, so to speak, working entirely behind the scenes through ordinary circumstances and ordinary actions of people—is even more important, because that is the way God usually works.**

For over a decade and in a variety of ways, God acted incognito to bring about His good, acceptable, and perfect will in Joseph's life. In the midst of incredible injustices, this young adult simply trusted God and did what was pleasing in His sight. Like the patriarch Joseph, at some point in time, you and I will have to decide what we believe about the sovereignty of God. Is God in total control or not? If He is, then we can unequivocally trust Him in all things. If He is not, then life is a glorious accident, and we should consider abandoning faith and finding our own way through this maze of life.

....

Take some time and clarify what you truly believe about the sovereignty of God.

Are you able to say with Job; "The LORD gave and the LORD has taken away; may the name of the LORD be praised"(Job 1:21)?

....

My friend Barb Dreyer taught me a valuable lesson regarding the Potter's sovereignty over the clay. Every time Barb fires her kiln, she designates two pieces out of approximately 70 pieces to the bagwell—one in the right side, the other in the left side. The bagwell is an area that fires at a hotter temperature than the rest of the kiln because the pieces are in separate chambers with the gas burner shooting directly at the pottery. While we unloaded her kiln, Barb gave special attention to these bagwell pieces and set them apart as incomparable. The dynamics of this intense firing create a color scheme and beauty that are unique and set apart from the rest of the wares in the kiln. In like manner, God chooses the clay, shapes it as He wills, places the vessels perfectly in the kiln, and fires them to completion. As the story of Joseph demonstrates, the Potter rules and overrules, including His sovereign choice of what pieces to place in the bagwell. His independent and meticulous placement has in mind our conformity to the glorious image of His Son Jesus Christ. Evangelist J. Wilbur Chapman provides valuable insight regarding this transformation process:

> **The clay is not attractive in itself, but when the hands of the potter touch it, and the thought of the potter is brought to bear upon it, and the plan of the potter is worked out in it and through it, then there is a real transformation.**

•••

Journal about a time when God turned up the heat of the kiln and sovereignly fired the clay of your life.

How did that experience feel and how did you respond?

Did that "bagwell" encounter result in a more beautiful vessel to the glory of the Potter and the good of the pot?

•••

Day 4

A Personal Touch

O ver the years, God has periodically tapped me on the shoulder to remind me of His loving and sovereign activity in my life. I often look back and find myself standing in awe of the Lord for His divine orchestration that has accomplished great things.

••

Write out Proverbs 16:9.

How does this biblical principle make you feel toward the Potter and the direction your life takes?

••

How grateful I am today that God directed me to the right when I wanted to go left. At times, He caused me to move forward when I desired to stand still. The Spirit of Jesus challenged me to take a break when I wanted to stay busy or take a risk when I wanted to play it safe. God has driven this proverb home time and again; however, a watershed experience goes back to my early encounters with Christ. Roughly four years after becoming a Christian, I sensed an overwhelming call to serve the Lord oversees as a vocational missionary. As a single, young adult, I planned to get my feet wet in missions by participating in a Discipleship Training School (DTS) with Last Days Ministries in Tyler, Texas. Upon completion of DTS, I would then serve on a two-year mission stint with Youth with a Mission (YWAM). I quit my job as a toolmaker, sold my house, and responded like Isaiah: "Here am I, send me!" (Isaiah 6:8). However, a few weeks before leaving for Texas, I broke the tibia and fibula of my left leg while playing soccer. Because of this injury and the practical nature of these ministry opportunities, I could not study at Last Days Ministries or serve with YWAM.

I found it incredibly hard to reconcile what God was doing through this injury. Remember, I "gave up" my career and home and said, "Anywhere You want me to go, Lord, I am available." Well, that sovereign act of God redirected the whole course of my life. God's planned detour led me to Bible school, where I majored in Bible and missions. During that time, the Lord clarified my call for vocational ministry and directed me to serve as a pastor, mobilizing the church for missions. Looking back, I thank God for revealing His perfect schematic for my life. I have jokingly said to the Lord, "You did not need to break my leg to get my attention." I sense the Potter responded by saying, "Keith, I wish that were the case." That major diversion God coordinated has brought much good over the years, for which I am incredibly grateful.

....

Describe a time when God totally redirected the course of your life and demonstrated His ways are best.

....

In his book, *Deep and Wide*, Andy Stanley shares a personal story about growing up as a pastor's kid. He describes how his father, Charles Stanley, learned that in life the only "predictable and unchanging component was the sovereignty of God." In 1969, Charles moved his family from Florida to serve as the senior associate minister at First Baptist Atlanta. He quickly discovered that the church was unhealthy, and within two years the deacons asked the senior pastor to leave. At the request of the pastoral search committee, Charles filled the pulpit while they pursued a new senior minister. Providentially, the church began to grow, baptisms and offerings increased, and spiritual life returned to the church. This progress began to disturb the power brokers, who did not consider Charles qualified for the senior position. His age, education, and preaching style all worked against him. Finally, the leadership asked him to step down from preaching and ultimately put pressure on him to resign. Reflecting on his father and that challenging time in ministry, Andy Stanley shares his father's wise words, "In those days, when I would look around at circumstances, everything said, 'Go.' But on my knees, I sensed God saying, 'You came here out of obedience to me. I'll let you know when it's time to leave.'"

Because of his spiritual resolve, things went from bad to worse for Charles Stanley and the leadership of the church. Charles learned firsthand what it meant to turn the other cheek when a board member actually punched him in the face during a business meeting. Leadership tried forcing his resignation, but when all efforts failed, it led to a business meeting where the deacons intended to vote him out of the church. Providentially, the vote failed by an overwhelming majority. Immediately, a motion from the floor came, nominating Charles for senior pastor. The deacons tried to end the meeting, but the grandson of the man who wrote *Robert's Rules of Order* was present and reminded the congregation of parliamentary procedures. The motion was seconded, and an overwhelming majority elected Charles Stanley as the senior pastor of First Baptist Atlanta. More than four decades have passed with Charles Stanley still filling the pulpit and leading the church. His life testifies to what John Newton taught about God's sovereignty many centuries ago:

> When [God] has a work to accomplish and his time is come, however inadequate and weak the means he employs may seem to a carnal eye, the success is infallibly secured: for all things serve him, and are in his hands as clay in the hands of a potter. Great and marvelous are thy works, Lord God Almighty! Just and true are thy ways, thou King of saints!

Take a moment and reflect on a time when God's sovereign hand changed the direction of your life. Looking back, can you see how that turn in the road accomplished God's loving and good purposes in your life? Have you expressed gratitude for His divine activity?

Being clay in the Potter's hands reminds us that God can do whatever He wants with us. However, He will always act in accordance with His character (2 Timothy 2:11–13). Therefore, we can trust the sovereign hands of the Potter to shape, mold, and make us into vessels of honor fit for His use. We must always remember that our wise God knows infinitely more than we do regarding any subject that we may consider ourselves experts. His desire for us is that we recognize Him as sovereign God and declare our absolute dependence on Him.

Is there anything in your life today that you need to relinquish to the sovereign will of the Potter?

Will you take time now to yield this particular area to the Potter through prayer and commitment?

Day 5
Learning to Trust

····················

Write out Proverbs 3:5–6.

Why is it so vital to your spiritual transformation to trust the Lord with every aspect of your life?

····················

On Easter of 2013 Nathan and Connie Backstrom joined our church family for worship and related their story of tragedy, broken hearts, and sorrow, but also of God's faithfulness, love, mercy, and forgiveness. The Backstroms remind us that life is unpredictable and that God has a way of intruding and leading us on a journey that we would never anticipate, even in our wildest dreams.

On the morning of October 10, 2004, a crisp, clear day started out quite ordinarily with Nathan and Connie taking their four youngest sons, Jacob (17), Justin (16), Ryan (12), and Charles (8) to church while their oldest son Matthew (20) went off to work. Nathan, a pilot with Northwest Airlines, had to fly out that morning, so he left church early. After worship, the Backstrom clan went home and enjoyed a light lunch. Later that afternoon, Justin asked his mother if he and Matthew could go to Walmart. Connie agreed, and Jacob joined his brothers. Before Matthew left, his mother looked at him and said, "Take good care of my boys." Matthew smiled and said, "I will." From the kitchen window, Connie waved good-bye as her sons drove away. Connie recalls looking at the kitchen clock; it was 4:36 p.m.

About 6:29 p.m., Matthew called to say they were leaving Target and heading for Walmart. At 7:20 p.m., the phone rang; it was Jacob, the detail man. He said, "Hi, Mom. We are leaving Walmart. What's for supper?"

Connie said, "Salmon. I just put it in the oven. It will be ready by the time you get home."

Depending on traffic, it would take 30 to 40 minutes to get from Walmart to the Backstrom house. When the boys were not home by 8:00 p.m., Connie was concerned, but not overly. Nathan checked in around 8:30 p.m., just before flying out that evening from Minneapolis.

He asked Connie how things were going, and she said, "Not good. The boys are not home yet, and they should have been home almost half an hour ago." When the boys did not show up by 9:00 p.m., Connie called Matthew's cell phone but got no response.

At 9:20 p.m., two hours after Connie had spoken with Jacob, she saw two sets of headlights coming up her driveway. Her first thought was, *Those buggers. They stopped to get their friend Mike and didn't bother to call me.* But, when Connie saw two sheriffs' cars in her driveway, she immediately knew that someone was dead.

The deputies asked Connie a few questions, and then the words that no parent should ever have to hear were spoken: "We are sorry to inform you that Matthew and Justin were killed in a crash near Farmington this evening. There was a third boy with them. Do you know who that would be?"

Connie replied, "That would be my son, Jacob."

The officer said, "Jacob is in critical condition and was taken to Regions Hospital for surgery."

Nathan still vividly remembers how he responded when Connie called him. "I laid down my phone and said, 'Dear Jesus, help me'—four simple words calling on the God of the universe. I've used that prayer many times since."

Connie began calling family and friends to ask for prayer for Jacob and to tell them that Matthew and Justin had been killed in a crash. She also called a friend to ask if she would come to stay with Ryan and Charles while she and Nathan went to the hospital to be with Jacob. As Connie waited, she saw state trooper Lieutenant Bob Meyerson walking to her door. She ran out the door and hugged him because Lieutenant Meyerson was a longstanding family friend. As Connie drove with Lieutenant Meyerson to the hospital, she thought, *God, this is too big to be just about us. What do You want me to do?* They met Nathan at the gas station and then rushed to Regions Hospital. When they arrived at the hospital, the doctors told them Jacob was out of surgery, on life support, and that his blood pressure was dangerously low. They were escorted to a waiting room on the surgical floor. Friends joined them, and a nurse came in to deliver a clear plastic bag with Jacob's bloody belongings. Connie thought, *I need to keep these. Kids need something tangible to understand how their actions impact others. Lord, I want to make a difference. I will not go where You do not open the door. This is Your work, and I do not have the energy to open even one door.*

The doctors told the Backstroms they could see Jacob. When they arrived at Jacob's hospital room that night, one of the first things they did was talk with the neurosurgeon who had performed the surgery early in the evening. First thing, and two times later, the Backstroms asked the surgeon about Jacob's condition and requested he be completely honest. Each time he answered saying Jacob was brain dead, no brain activity whatsoever.

When they walked into Jacob's room, they found him under a white heating blanket, eyes wide open, fully dilated and staring at the ceiling. When Connie saw Jacob like that, her only thought was, *He's not here. He's gone.* Jacob was very cold to the touch; he was in a neck brace; and tubes were coming out of his head, trying to relieve the pressure on his brain. His blood pressure was very low, so they decided to check his brain waves again, but he had none. Then his heart started shutting down, so they sent for the paddles. Connie asked, "Why? He's gone. Let him go with his brothers." As they stood there, surrounded by friends and church family, they prayed and sang.

After saying good-bye to Jacob, Lieutenant Meyerson took the Backstroms to the Dakota County Morgue to identify and say good-bye to Matthew and Justin. Their hearts breaking, they went home. For the next three nights, Connie slept with Jacob's bloodstained clothing. It was all she had left of her precious son. The following day, the Backstrom home was full of family and friends, and their lawn inundated with media. Ryan vividly remembers how his parents took immediate action with news reporters. Right away, they began sharing Christ through this tragedy; they took what could have destroyed them and turned it into something that could spread the gospel.

I had the privilege of meeting Connie and Nathan in the winter of 2013 in Apple Valley, Minnesota. During our time together, I sensed that although eight years had passed, the "hard work of grieving"—a phrase Connie used while sharing her testimony that Easter Sunday—continued to take place. They spoke much of God's love and how He chose to use them for His glory. Connie reflected on how "you can't fix what happened, but you can trust that God was in control and that He is sovereign."

Nathan shared an inspirational story that captures the Potter's hand-iwork in a marvelous way. Nathan regularly took his boys out for a meal and would ask them 21 questions—fun stuff like, "What is your favorite movie?" or, "What is your most embarrassing moment?" The question-ing culminated with dad asking his boys, "How do you want your life to count for eternity?" Nathan remembers Jacob saying, "I want to win 20 people to faith in Christ." Looking back God honored Jacob's desire, because his death opened the door to prison ministry, high school assemblies, youth events, Teen Challenge outreach, and church min-istry. Throughout the years, the Backstroms have spoken at hundreds of events and thousands have been influenced for Christ. God took the brokenness of this dear family and brought His priceless treasure of the gospel to many. At our Easter worship, where Connie and Nathan gave their testimony, dozens of individuals made first-time professions of faith in Christ. To God be the glory.

••

If Nathan and Connie did not have a biblical view of God's sovereignty, where do you think they would be today?

What lessons can we learn from this dear family's experience on how to trust the sovereign work and will of the Potter in our lives?

••

Day 6
God's Sovereignty and Calvary

A few months after the crash, the Backstroms received an autopsy report and learned about the nature of their sons' violent deaths. That information hurt them deeply, and Connie cried out to the Lord, saying, "My boys were good boys. They did not deserve to die such violent deaths." That, of course, was the honest declaration of a mother who deeply loved her sons. In a quiet but loving and gracious way, God responded, "My Son did not deserve to die, either, but I sent Him anyway." The Bible offers no clearer picture of God's sovereignty than the death, burial, and Resurrection of Jesus Christ from the grave.

....

Read Acts 2:22–24. How does Peter address the tension between the sovereignty of God and human responsibility as he describes the Crucifixion of Christ?

Read Acts 2:36. What was God's grand purpose for the death, burial, and Resurrection of Jesus Christ?

Read John 10:17–18. How does Jesus describe His sacrificial death?

....

The clay of Jesus' life was soft, pure, and moldable in the Potter's hand. His submissive attitude resulted in His becoming "obedient to death— even death on a cross!" (Philippians 2:8). These redemptive truths remind us that Calvary is not a mistake. The death, burial, and Resurrection of Jesus Christ is not plan B. From eternity past, God chose to give His Son as a ransom for many (Mark 10:45). Jesus is the voluntary and obedient lamb slain from the foundation of the world (Revelation 13:8).

Today, Connie and Nathan Backstrom can rest in the Potter's hands because they know Justin, Jacob, and Matthew had a personal relationship with Jesus Christ and are now in the presence of their Lord and Savior. Their prayer is that the death of their three precious sons will continue to impact lives for eternity.

So, have you yielded your life to the Master Potter through Jesus Christ His Son? Do you recognize that the clay of your life is marred, and that there is no possible way for you to purify it on your own? Will you embrace His grace and allow the Potter to remake you into the image and likeness of His Son? Be honest with the Potter about the impurities in your clay. Confess your sins; He is faithful and just to forgive and cleanse you from past, present, and future wrongdoings. Thank the Potter for His forgiveness and for purifying the clay of your life. Now that He is both Lord and Savior of your life, ask Him to shape you into a vessel of honor, fit for His use.

When I put my trust in Christ, a pastor helped me express my desire to relinquish my life to the Lord. If God's Spirit is working in your heart, and you desire to call upon the name of the Lord and be saved, I encourage you to look toward heaven and pray this prayer of faith.

Father,
I thank You for loving me, especially because
You know how marred the clay of my life truly is. I thank
You for sending Your Son Jesus Christ to pay the penalty for
every impurity, crack, and break in the clay of my life. I recognize my
sin has prevented fellowship with You. Today, I repent
of my sins and put my faith in Jesus Christ as my Savior
and Lord. Thank You for complete forgiveness through
Jesus Christ my Lord. In Jesus' name, I pray.
Amen.

Recommended Resources

Books form us, dynamically molding our minds, and shaping our souls. Therefore, reading the best material is not only wise but also vital to growing in the grace and knowledge of our Lord and Savior Jesus Christ. This bibliography includes some of the resources that have influenced my writing of *Living Clay*. I hope you will find them, like I did, to be spiritually transformational.

Apologetics

The Case for Faith by Lee Strobel

How Can I Know? by Robert Jeffress

Is God Really in Control? by Joni Earekson Tada

Is God Really in Control? Trusting God in a World of Hurt by Jerry Bridges

The Gift of Pain by Philip Yancey and Dr. Paul Brand

What's So Amazing about Grace? by Philip Yancey

What's So Great about Christianity by Dinesh D'Souza

Where Is God When It Hurts? by Philip Yancey

Archaeology and History

A History of Israel by John Bright

Jeremiah: An Archaeological Companion by Philip J. King

Order and History, Volume I: Israel and Revelation by Eric Voegelin

Christian Growth

Amazing Grace: 366 Inspiring Hymn Stories for Daily Devotions by Kenneth W. Osbeck

Fearless by Max Lucado

The Grace Awakening by Charles Swindoll

Grace Grows Best in Winter by Margaret Clarkson

The Grand Weaver by Ravi Zacharias

The Imitation of Christ by Thomas à Kempis

It Only Hurts on Monday by Gary L. McIntosh and Robert L. Edmondson

Margin by Richard A. Swenson

Pursued by Jud Wilhite

The Root of the Righteous by A. W. Tozer

Weird by Craig Groeschel

Commentaries

1–2 Timothy and Titus: To Guard the Deposit
    by R. Kent Hughes and Bryan Chapell

Be Comforted by Warren W. Wiersbe

Be Decisive by Warren W. Wiersbe

Be Holy by Warren W. Wiersbe

The Bible Reader's Companion, Your Guide to Every Chapter of the Bible
    by Lawrence O. Richards

The Book of Jeremiah by John A. Thompson

A Commentary on the Book of the Prophet Jeremiah by William L. Holladay

Exposition of the Epistle of James and the Epistles of John
    by Simon J. Kistemaker

Jeremiah 1–20 by Jack R. Lundbom

Jeremiah and Lamentations by R. K. Harrison

Jeremiah, Lamentations: An Exegetical and Theological Exposition of Holy
    Scripture by F. B. Huey

Life Application Bible Commentary: 1 & 2 Corinthians edited by Grant Osborne
    and Philip W. Comfort

Opening Up Psalms by Roger Ellsworth

World Biblical Commentary, Volume 20: Psalms 51–100 by Marvin E. Tate

Discipleship

Bruchko by Bruce Olson

The Complete Book of Discipleship by Bill Hull

Let Your Life Speak: Listening for the Voice of Vocation by Parker Palmer

A Long Obedience in the Same Direction by Eugene Peterson

Making Sense of Suffering by Joni Eareckson Tada

Ordering Your Private World by Gordon MacDonald

A Place of Healing: Wrestling With the Mysteries of Suffering, Pain, and
    God's Sovereignty by Joni Eareckson Tada

Ravished by Beauty: The Surprising Legacy of Reformed Spirituality
    by Belden C. Lane

Sovereignty by Joni Eareckson Tada

The Ten Commandments from the Back Side by J. Ellsworth Kalas

The Tozer Topical Reader by A. W. Tozer and compiled by Ron Eggert

Leadership

The Carrot Principle by Adrian Gostick and Chester Elton

Courageous Leadership by Bill Hybels

Decision Points by George W. Bush

Deep and Wide by Andy Stanley

Emotionally Healthy Church by Peter Scazzero

Emotionally Healthy Leadership by Peter Scazzero

Great Souls by David Aikman

Leading On Empty by Wayne Cordeiro

Liberating Ministry from the Success Syndrome by Kent and Barbara Hughes

Preaching to Convince by James D. Berkley

Lexicons and Dictionaries

Dictionary of Biblical Languages with Semantic Domains: Hebrew by James A. Swanson

Greek-English Lexicon of the New Testament: Based on Semantic Domains edited by J. P. Louw and Eugene Albert Nida

Theological Wordbook of the Old Testament by R. Laird Harris, Gleason L. Archer Jr., and Bruce K. Waltke

Word Studies from the Greek New Testament by Kenneth S. Wuest

Potter and Clay

30 Days in the Potter's House by Douglas Marks

The Complete Potter by Steve Mattison

Impressions in Clay by Wendy Lawton

Worthy Vessels by Nell Kennedy

Soul Care

Crazy Busy by Kevin DeYoung

Emotionally Healthy Spirituality by Peter Scazzero

Perspectives on the Sabbath by Charles Arand, Craig Blomberg, Skip Maccarty, and Joseph Pipa

Resilient Ministry by Bob Burns, Tasha Chapman, and Donald Guthrie

The Rest of God: Restoring Your Soul by Restoring Sabbath by Mark Buchanan

Sabbath by Dan B. Allender

Soul Keeping by John Ortberg

Spiritual Rhythm by Mark Buchanan

Spiritual Disciplines

Celebration of Discipline by Richard Foster

The Spirit of the Disciplines by Dallas Willard

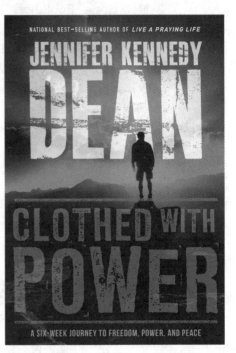

New Hope® Publishers is a division of WMU®, an international organization that challenges Christian believers to understand and be radically involved in God's mission. For more information about WMU, go to wmu.com. More information about New Hope books may be found at NewHopePublishers.com. New Hope books may be purchased at your local bookstore.

Please go to
NewHopePublishers.com
for more helpful information about
Living Clay.

If you've been blessed by this book,
we would like to hear your story.
The publisher and author welcome your comments
and suggestions at: newhopereader@wmu.org.